# trellises
## & ARBORS

by Steve Cory and the Editors of Sunset Books, Menlo Park, California

## SUNSET BOOKS

VP, EDITORIAL DIRECTOR
Bob Doyle

DIRECTOR OF SALES
Brad Moses

DIRECTOR OF OPERATIONS
Rosann Sutherland

MARKETING MANAGER
Linda Barker

ART DIRECTOR
Vasken Guiragossian

## STAFF FOR THIS BOOK

SENIOR EDITOR
Carrie Dodson Davis

TEXT EDITOR
Esther R. Ferington

CONSULTANTS
Jacob Porter
Conrad Wennerberg

ILLUSTRATOR
Greg Maxson

PRODUCTION SPECIALISTS
Linda M. Bouchard
Janie Farn

PREPRESS COORDINATOR
Eligio Hernández

PROOFREADER
Denise Griffiths

INDEXER
Marjorie Joy

10 9 8 7 6 5 4 3 2 1
First Printing January 2008.
Copyright © 2008, Sunset Publishing
Corporation, Menlo Park, CA 94025.
Third edition. All rights reserved, including
the right of reproduction in whole or in part
in any form.
ISBN-13: 978-0-376-01797-0
ISBN-10: 0-376-01797-X
Library of Congress Control Number: 2007932163
Printed in the United States of America.

**COVER**
Photo by Russ Widstrand; design by Marlene Salon
in collaboration with Susan Hoover.

For additional copies of *Trellises & Arbors* or any
other Sunset book, visit us at www.sunsetbooks.com.

For more exciting home and garden ideas, visit
**myhomeideas**.com

*contents*

# SIMPLE CHARMS

ONE OF LIFE'S MORE SATISFYING PURSUITS is to build something by hand, perhaps with the help of a family member or friend, and then enjoy it for years to come. This is especially true in the garden, where nature's color palette will complement the beauty of your handiwork. Building an outdoor structure can be as small or as large a project as you want, and there are designs in this book suited to every skill level. All of them allow you to get creative and imbue your garden with some good old-fashioned charm. Just start with a design that's to your tastes, customize it with a favorite paint color or fanciful accessory, and top it off with your choice of climbing plant.

This book gives all the information you need to end up with the trellis or arbor that's just right for you. Begin with Chapter 1, where you'll see how stylish and innovative outdoor structures can take a garden space to the next level.

The do-it-yourself chapters that follow contain 40 trellis and arbor projects, from a fan design to dress up the side of your house to a cheerful archway perfect for welcoming guests. Each project begins with a description of the structure and how to get ready for building it. A materials list shows what you'll need from your local home center, and a detailed drawing explains how the pieces fit together. Clear, concise instructions with full-color photos expertly guide you every step of the way.

The next chapter, Choosing the Right Plants, offers Sunset's top 40 picks. Each entry specifies how the plant will grow on your structure, and gives tips to keep it thriving and healthy. No matter how green your thumb, you'll find this mini-encyclopedia of climbing vines very handy.

The last chapter offers expert advice on everything from choosing lumber to ensuring a lasting paint job. These pro pointers are useful in a broad range of building applications, and will help you complete your project safely and with a high level of craftsmanship.

So start imagining, designing, and building your project today! Whether it's a straightforward rectangle of latticework to support your favorite heirloom roses, or a gated arch that guides the way from the garage to the house, a trellis or arbor is sure to add simple, functional charm to your outdoor living space.

# going vertical
## in the garden

FLIP THROUGH THESE PAGES TO SEE ALL THE WAYS THAT TRELLISES AND ARBORS CAN TAKE A GARDEN FROM FLAT TO FABULOUS. FIND INSPIRATION FOR YOUR OWN YARD, FROM STYLISH OBELISKS THAT SEND PLANTS SKYWARD TO HANDSOME AND PRACTICAL STRUCTURES THAT OFFER SHADE AND SEATING.

# A SENSE OF STYLE

ARCHITECTURAL ELEMENTS GO A LONG WAY TOWARD ESTABLISHING A GARDEN'S STYLE, perhaps more so than the plants that grow up and around them. So before settling on a design for your trellis or arbor, consider the personality of your garden—or the personality you'd like it to have. Is it an exotic, junglelike oasis where you can get lost for an afternoon behind palm leaves and screens of bamboo? Or is it tidy and structured, with defined areas for sitting, gardening, and strolling? Choose a structure design that will give your outdoor space a cohesive look in the style of your choice. The following pages show how trellises and arbors can set the stage for several popular themes.

ABOVE: A mishmash of birdhouses pops up against simple panels of lattice. Delphinium, phlox, and yarrow stand tall in the foreground.

## Cottage Chic

Trellises and arbors are perhaps most at home in cottage-style gardens, where plants are free to wander and mingle. By giving plants a vertical dimension to latch onto, your garden will gain heightened layers of lushness, resulting in a spontaneous, exuberant look characteristic of cottage style. And forget the meticulous touch-up paint on these structures in a cottage garden: Often, the more weathered and shabby they look, the better they fit into the landscape.

ABOVE: A scallop-shaped arbor teeming with clematis offers a welcome twist on the classic rounded arch. Inside the garden, stalks of hollyhock and salvia dance behind neat rows of violas and boxwood.

RIGHT: A pine tree hugs a simple roofed arbor topped by a layer of woven reeds. Above the front opening, a wreath of metal leaves takes the place of living climbers. The spruce green paint takes its cue from the surrounding foliage and distinguishes the arbor from the fence running behind it.

FAR RIGHT: Two terra-cotta containers support a sturdy steel arch covered with apricot-pink roses, forming a portal to a hidden seating nook.

OPPOSITE: A well-worn arbor bench lends a patina of age to this cottage garden and gives guests a place to sit during their explorations.

## A Bit More Formal

A formal garden doesn't have to mean perfectly pruned parterres and Versailles-like topiaries. You can add a sense of refinement without a pair of manicuring scissors and a host of professional gardeners. Just look for ways to create a focal point, repeat interesting elements, or incorporate symmetry into your landscape. Combined with the right mix of plants, a unique trellis or strategically placed arbor may be all you need to dress up the outdoors.

LEFT: A crisp white gated arbor is the clear center of attention against a green palette of lawn, trees, and shrubs. Slate squares march two by two from the structure, challenging visitors to a match on the tennis court beyond.

OPPOSITE: Despite their straightforward construction, a series of classic obelisks introduce formality to a rural country-side. Standing in soldierly rows, the bare trellises make a pleasing, slightly austere statement against a sea of vivid green plantings.

RIGHT: In this stunning garden, years of pruning and training have resulted in row upon row of flourishing firethorn (*Pyracantha* 'Mohave') against the rear wall. Espalier—training a tree or shrub to grow along a wall—is a striking variation on the trellis idea that richly repays the skill, patience, and maintenance it requires of the gardener.

LEFT: An unadorned arbor serves as the backbone to this modestly proportioned garden, framing a row of dark green arborvitae. The natural color of the wooden structure links it to the prominent large clay urn. Lavender, astilbe, and ornamental grasses along a gravel path keep things from feeling stiff.

LEFT: A bamboo screen with trellis window both hides and reveals the landscape beyond, enhancing the mystery and interest of the space. Bamboo is a prized material in traditional Asian gardens because of its strength and resilience.

RIGHT: This Japanese-style tea garden features a series of raised beds—thresholds meant to help visitors leave daily stresses behind. An interesting composition of lath on the sides of the handsome arbor at center proves that latticework doesn't always have to be the traditional square or diamond pattern.

BELOW, LEFT: This driftwood and bamboo arbor adorned with hanging plants, wind chimes, and a brass bell is a creative, rustic take on the traditionally polished and manicured Asian garden. Splashy plantings and concrete steps and statuettes dot a bed of Irish moss.

BELOW, RIGHT: The classic upturned pagoda roofline on a wide arbor gate structure gives this woody garden an undeniably Asian aesthetic.

## Asian Flair

Asian gardens traditionally offer a sense of serenity and a space to reconnect with the natural world. An Asian-style aesthetic works well in a small space because it emphasizes judicious use of the land. Layered elements like trellises, arbors, raised beds, plantings, and garden pools maximize each square foot as they create a tranquil refuge from the everyday.

Here, an elaborate gate entrance is topped with glazed ceramic Japanese roof tiles and flanked by a wall inlaid with a trellis of bamboo lattice. Heavy metal-studded doors open onto a hammered bronze gong.

Mexican soda-pop bottles dangle from this 8-foot-square steel ramada, wrapped with concrete-reinforcing wire on the sides and top to offer climbing support to queen's wreath and other vines. Purple panels hung with a mirror and Corona beer trays form a funky backdrop to this perfect fiesta spot.

Hand-painted signs point the way to destinations as close as the front door and as far as Saigon. Four-by-four posts, painted purple, offer enough support for a heavy draping of wisteria.

BELOW: An outdoor museum display is born from a concrete bust and pedestal set amid a rich green grove. The art piece gains prominence from an inexpensive lattice panel crested with a decorative scroll.

## Eclectic Mix

The most interesting outdoor spaces are often formed by blending elements from a variety of sources and styles, creating a look that's all your own. Outdoor structures can be fashioned from and adorned with almost anything. A current trend is to create the feeling of an indoor room out of doors—so bring those collections and objets d'art from your fireplace mantel or bookshelf into the light of day! Or use found objects—anything from farm equipment that's fallen into disrepair to scraps of ornamental tile—to decorate your trellis or arbor.

LEFT: Stained glass and a small beaded chandelier add fanciful refinement to this rustic structure. The covered arbor and built-in bench, made from rough tree trunks and branches, seem to have grown out of the ground.

Tidy tucked-in branches make this arbor a neat match to the low boxwood hedges at its sides. Layers of delicate leaves all around it complete the autumnal tapestry.

## Twiggy and Branchy

Structures formed from branches are an obvious fit for natural- or rustic-style gardens, but they can also be interesting focal points in tropical or Asian designs. Because it's made of natural pieces, each creation is truly one of a kind, lending your landscape an authentic, hand-hewn look. See pages 50–52 for more detailed information on creating bentwood structures.

RIGHT: Herbaceous clematis finds support on a small woven tepee. Clay tiles lean against the base of the structure to provide shade to the burgeoning plant's roots.

FAR RIGHT: Arched branches nailed to a fence support golden hops (*Humulus lupulus* 'Aureus'), adding interest to what could have been a dull part of the garden.

Help kids build their own playhouse by putting those branches you just pruned to work. Here, gourd-shaped birdhouses ensure that plenty of feathered friends stop by for a visit.

BELOW: Structures built with natural components don't have to be small and quaint. This extravagant arbor made from cut and peeled cedar poles stretches alongside a garden pool toward a gazebo. The curved branches that form the roof and side arches were nailed into place right after cutting, when wood is most flexible.

# STRUCTURES WITH PURPOSE

WHILE GARDEN STRUCTURES CAN BE PURELY DECORATIVE (an iron obelisk punctuating a group of shorter plantings, for example), most offer an opportunity for form to meet function. A strategically placed arbor invites you to explore the path it spans, or to enjoy a glass of iced tea in the shade it provides. A lattice fence makes a pretty backdrop to your container plants, and also keeps the dog from getting out. Attaching a gate to an arbor or hinging a panel of lattice fencing adds even more utility (see pages 111–113 for tips on gate construction). In short, a well-designed garden structure with a clear sense of purpose can make your outdoor space infinitely more livable.

A geometric pattern of pavers proves an interesting counterpoint to the canopy of the branch-built arbor overhead. Climbing roses and foliage are vital to achieving the lush, tunnel-like effect.

## Walkways

Perhaps an arbor's most natural purpose is as an inviting portal into the garden, clearly heralding the entryway to visitors. Multiply the effect with a longer tunnel arbor or a series of arbors. Just make sure to maintain a balanced proportion between the structure and the walkway it spans. If you are framing a narrow dirt path, for instance, 12-foot-wide archways would destroy the intimacy of the trail. Likewise, the shape and material of the arbor should complement the path below it. See page 92 for instructions on building a dramatic 4-foot-wide arched arbor, perfect for leading the way to your favorite garden spot.

**ABOVE:** Iron arches reaching 12 feet tall and set 8 feet apart host a garden spectacular, especially in April, when the clematis and roses are in full bloom. The width of the structure allows plenty of room for alliums, pincushion flowers, and nepeta to spill onto the sand and gravel pathway without hindering foot traffic.

**RIGHT:** This simple, serviceable arbor bridge has an understated charm all its own. Ornamental grapevine covers the overhead portion and container plants complement the benches.

**OPPOSITE:** A simple curving path connects two elegant garden structures, both dressed in wedding-day white. With plenty of manicured lawn on either side of the path for folding chairs, it's hard to imagine a more ideal set-up for a marriage ceremony.

LEFT: Plants and planting tools alike hang from diamond-patterned lath panels nailed to the backside of a fence. A tiled worktable completes this potting area.

RIGHT: This terraced garden gains definition and interest from a series of arched trellises connected overhead. Bright pink roses planted in raised brick borders pop against the olive green of the woodwork.

BELOW: Here, three walls of lattice abutting a house define a courtyard, while an arched arbor grants entry. The lattice trellis sits atop a foundation of bricks for a more polished look (and by avoiding ground contact, the wood is less prone to rotting).

## Fences and Dividers

Fences can take design cues from trellises and arbors to define a space in a decorative, interesting way. Lattice is a common choice because it offers a measure of privacy without blocking light and airflow. By varying the pattern and positioning of the lath, a trellis fence can complement any style while adding ornamentation to your space. Bring plants into the mix, and you've got living vertical planes that gracefully define and contain different areas of your garden.

ABOVE: In an expansive yard that flows into the open space beyond, a fenced-in area like this one offers the chance to plant a more intimate, structured garden safe from local fauna looking for a snack. Painted country blue to match the fence, gazebos with diamond-shaped latticework accent each corner of the enclosure, shading benches where visitors can sit and enjoy the view.

RIGHT: A rounded arch mirrors the U-shaped cutout in the adjoining fence, creating a circular window between a private backyard and a public garden strip blooming with astilbe. The unique character of the cutout and the amount of light it lends to the shady yard are worth the slight loss of privacy to the homeowners.

## A Nice Spot to Sit

Arbors with built-in seats, swings, or hammocks issue regular reminders to settle in and enjoy your garden. A shady bench arbor sumptuously covered in roses, for instance, invites you to put down your trowel and pick up a glass of lemonade instead. Placing an arbor along the landscape's perimeter, rather than front and center, will offer more tranquility and shade, while adding interest to an otherwise muted section of the garden.

LEFT: 'Cécile Brünner', a fairly vigorous rose, is supported by a classic arched arbor. Each side of the structure has cozy seating surrounded by lattice panels to support the rose canes and provide backrests. To discourage rot, the arbor rests on a patio of bricks that keeps its wood base off the ground.

BELOW: Bougainvillea is at its best on this store-bought metal arbor. The aqua blue of the bench cushions is the perfect color complement to the bright pink blooms.

ABOVE: The broad U-shaped bench in this arbor creates a space that's perfect for sharing a board game, a cool drink, or a conversation.

RIGHT: 'Pink Morning Jewel' rose adorns an arbor bench set within an elaborate display of rose bushes. The unique tiered shape of the bench's overhead keeps the structure from feeling ordinary.

The amenities found under this patio roof rival those of any indoor room. Mission-style graces the tiled fireplace surround, hanging pendant lamps, and the shape of the structure's lower crossbeams. Guests have their choice of sitting at the dining table, where they can enjoy food fresh off the neighboring rotisserie, or in front of the fire; both spots encourage them to kick off their shoes and stick their toes in the sand.

## Outdoor Rooms

If you're looking for stylish ways to extend your living space out of doors, consider a gazebo, patio roof, or pergola—all more elaborate versions of the arbor. These larger structures provide partial shelter from sun, wind, and weather, and visually frame outdoor rooms perfect for every activity from barbecuing to bocce ball. Add comfy furniture or a portable firepit (s'mores, anyone?), and you'll be reluctant to ever go back in the house.

RIGHT: An overhead positioned right off the house makes a smooth transition from indoors to out, and offers a pleasant place to dine outside. A canopy of leafy vines permits just the right amount of filtered light to reach the patio below.

BELOW: This Yorkshire terrier has the right idea, spending a sunny afternoon on a wide chaise longue. A custom metal structure defines this personal-size sanctuary without obstructing any views of the surrounding garden.

# ALL ABOUT THE PLANTS

WHILE A BARE TRELLIS OR ARBOR CAN ADD A DECORATIVE QUALITY TO A GARDEN, clothing it in plants turns the piece into living sculpture. A vertical structure teeming in vibrant clematis or painted red with Virginia creeper becomes a natural element integrated into the surrounding landscape, and adds visual interest by bringing plant life skywards. If you have a specific plant preference, choose the right design to support it—strong enough for the weight of the full-grown plant, but not so big that it dwarfs a wispy, delicate growth. For more ways to achieve plant/structure harmony, turn to page 120.

The climbing rose 'Mme. Isaac Pereire', with its gorgeously fragrant blooms and long, flexible canes, is a perfect fit for this branchy tripod trellis.

OPPOSITE: An elegant arbor screen sets the stage for the abundance of jewels in this garden—thriving alchemilla, salvia, iris, and nepeta, to name a few. The wide lattice of the structure itself provides good air circulation to the climbing rose 'Zephirine Drouhin', helping to prevent the powdery mildew that often plagues this variety.

RIGHT: Perennial morning glories and potato vine spill onto a yellow stucco arbor that would make an idyllic entrance to any Tuscan villa. Metal grids placed behind the arbor are the real support structure for these twining vines, which need slender rods to coil onto.

This abundant front-yard garden offers the home a veil of privacy from the street. On the arbor, lime-green leaves of golden hop (*Humulus lupulus* 'Aureus') mingle with wine-colored clematis *(Clematis jackmanii)* for an intoxicating effect.

ABOVE: A mixture of wall and freestanding trellises makes the most of a cook's garden space. The woven willow arches support sugar snap peas.

# Edible Climbers

Going vertical with edibles not only adds growing space (more room for your favorite heirloom tomatoes!), but also produces a greater harvest: The fruits will be easier to see and pick and they won't come in contact with the ground, where they might rot. Put up your stakes and trellises at planting time; staking plants after they have begun to sprawl risks disturbing the roots and breaking the stems. Among the prettiest vining edibles are beans, grapes, nasturtiums, peas, and squash.

OPPOSITE: Long and quirky *Zucchetta rampicante*, an Italian heirloom squash, is sure to put a smile on anyone's face. This vigorous zucchini needs strong support, like this series of tall metal arches.

BELOW, LEFT: An 8-foot-tall cedar arbor is just the right height for picking a sweet, juicy 'Thompson Seedless'. The container-grown table grapes were planted at each corner of the structure one April, and six months later they covered the arbor. The vines began producing fruit in the second summer. In colder regions, consider hardier varieties like 'Edelweiss' or 'Interlaken'.

BELOW, RIGHT: Climbing beans don't need fancy digs; three sticks tied together at the top with twine will suffice. Wrap the tepee with netting for a dense cover of leaves.

# trellis
# projects

# PREMADE TRELLISES

MANY IMPRESSIVE-LOOKING TRELLIS STRUCTURES are not built from scratch by a woodworker or a homeowner, but purchased in kit form from a manufacturer. If you type "trellis" into a search engine, you will find a good number of companies that offer attractive and easy-to-assemble trellises (as well as arbors; see pages 74–75).

## Buying and Assembly

Choose products that will last. If you want a wood structure, look for rot-resistant materials such as Western red cedar and mahogany. All joints should be not only nailed or stapled, but also glued. Stakes and fasteners should be made of stainless steel or aluminum; galvanized fasteners may rust after a few years. Expect to apply stain and sealer to protect against rot, especially if the trellis will get wet for prolonged periods. Vinyl trellises are rot-proof, but any galvanized fasteners need to be protected with clear sealer or they may rust.

**Assembly.** Some units are complete out of the box, while others need simple assembly—perhaps driving screws through predrilled holes. You may need to install small hinges. Position them so only the pin portion is exposed, and drive the small screws.

**This charming wooden lattice panel with oval cutout and decorative posts arrives on your doorstep as a kit; assembly and installation instructions are included.**

**Staking.** If your trellis comes with metal stakes, drive them into the ground next to the rear of framing members until the arrow-shaped flanges disappear into the ground. Drive short decking screws through the stakes and into the trellis. If no stakes are provided, make your own: Rip-cut cedar 1-by lumber so it is a bit narrower than the framing member it will hide behind, and cut a point at the end. Drive the stake and drill pilot holes before fastening it to the trellis with screws.

### Attaching to a wall.

Some trellises come with plastic spacers and screws. If yours doesn't, cut pieces of copper or plastic pipe. (The CPVC pipe used here has a beige color that blends better than white PVC pipe.) Drive screws into wood siding. If you have a masonry wall, use masonry shields (see pages 35 and 41).

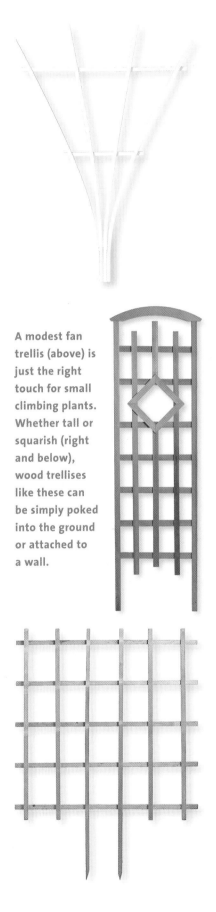

A modest fan trellis (above) is just the right touch for small climbing plants. Whether tall or squarish (right and below), wood trellises like these can be simply poked into the ground or attached to a wall.

### The metal alternative.

If you buy a metal trellis, look for a powder or poly coating, rather than simple paint. Check the joints and the ends, where the coating may not be complete and where rust is most likely to develop; if necessary, hit these spots with dabs of rust-resistant paint.

# SIMPLE WALL TRELLIS

THERE IS NOTHING LIKE A TRELLIS FOR DRESSING UP AN EXPANSE OF BLANK WALL. Any wall, whether it is part of your house, garden shed, or garage, can provide a backdrop for a lovely array of climbing plants. Of course, plants on a south-facing trellis will produce the most flowers and the lushest foliage, but many do well even with a northern exposure.

A trellis like this one, made with simple 2 by 2 framing, is ideal for mounting against a wall. If you want a freestanding trellis, you'll need a stouter structure (see pages 42 and following).

## Getting Ready

This project can be built and attached to a wall in several hours, though you'll have to wait for the paint to dry. The grid is made of vinyl lattice, which won't splinter or rot and never needs painting. The frame is made of treated 2 by 2s that are well protected with several coats of primer and paint. Because the back of the trellis will not be visible, it can simply be screwed onto the frame, with no molding pieces to cover the edges. The trellis shown here is 32 by 66 inches, but you can adjust the size to suit your situation. If your trellis is wider than 48 inches or taller than 96 inches, you will need to use two pieces of lattice and cover the joint with trim.

Work on a flat surface, such as a sheet of plywood on two sawhorses or a garage floor. This will help keep the finished structure flat as well.

## Materials List

- Three 8' 2 × 2s
- Sheet of vinyl lattice
- 1¹/₄" decking or stainless-steel screws
- ¹/₂" copper or plastic pipe
- Lag screws and shields (for masonry walls)
- Exterior primer and paint

## PRO TIP

Once plants start growing onto a trellis, it will be difficult, if not impossible, to repaint or restain it without damaging the climbing plants. So take the time now to apply a thick protective coating.

**1** **CUT THE HALF-LAP JOINTS.** Cut two 2 by 2 pieces 6 inches longer than the width of the trellis, and two more pieces 6 inches longer than its height. The pieces will be joined with half-lap joints (see pages 152–153). To mark for the notches, clamp the four pieces together, aligned at one end. Hold a scrap 2 by 2 and mark for $1\frac{1}{2}$-inch-wide notches beginning 3 inches from the ends. Set a circular saw to a depth of $\frac{3}{4}$ inch; test it on a scrap 2 by 2 to make sure you will cut exactly halfway through. Carefully cut each notch line, then make a series of closely spaced cuts in between. Clean out the middle with a chisel and hammer. (You can also use a router; see page 153.) Test to see that a 2 by 2 fits snugly in each notch without having to pound it in.

**2** **BUILD THE FRAME.** Prime and paint the 2 by 2s; slap plenty of paint into the cut joints, which are porous. After the paint dries, assemble the parts. Use a framing square or two factory edges of a plywood sheet to make sure the corners are square. Drill a pilot hole and drive a screw into each joint.

**3** **CUT THE LATTICE TO FIT.** Place the lattice sheet on top of the frame, with two edges flush with the edges of the frame. Use a felt-tip marker to mark the sheet at the other corners for cutting, then mark the cut lines using a straight board. Set a circular saw to cut $\frac{1}{4}$ inch deeper than the lattice thickness, and position boards underneath the lattice on either side of a cut line, as shown. Cut freehand or use a clamped straight-edge, such as the factory edge of a plywood sheet, as a guide (see page 145).

**4** **FASTEN THE LATTICE.** Drive $1\frac{1}{4}$-inch screws to fasten the lattice to the back of the frame. (These screws will not be visible when the trellis is installed.)

**5** **ATTACH TO THE WALL.** Cut six or eight $2\frac{1}{2}$-inch-long pieces of copper or plastic pipe to hold the trellis away from the wall. To anchor to a masonry wall, use lag screws and shields (see page 41). Drive screws to attach to a wood surface.

# WALL PANEL

THIS TALL, WALL-ATTACHED TRELLIS PANEL IS ELEGANTLY SIMPLE. You may want to build several and space them one panel's width apart, as shown at left.

For a trellis like this, the exact dimensions of the pieces can make a big difference in the overall appearance. We show lattice that is ³/₄ inch thick and 1¹/₈ inches wide. You could use standard 1 by 2s, which are ³/₄ inch by 1¹/₂ inches, but the result would be surprisingly clunky-looking. Rip-cutting the slats will take only a half hour or so.

## Getting Ready

There are no half-lap joints, so this project can be built quickly. Start by rip-cutting the lattice slats and frame pieces. Because the trellis will be attached to the house, the frame need not be very strong and can be assembled with a single screw at each joint. Since both vertical and horizontal pieces run around the perimeter of the lattice, the frame can be simply attached.

The grid shown here is 68 by 22 inches, but you could widen or lengthen it. If you widen it by more than 8 inches, add another vertical lattice piece. Here we use cedar, but you could use treated lumber, which can be stained or painted.

## Materials List

- Two 6' 1 × 6s for lattice slats and cap rail
- Two 8' ⁵/₄ × 6s for the frame
- 4" decking or stainless-steel screws; 1¹/₄" and 2¹/₂" galvanized nails or staples
- ¹/₂" copper or plastic pipe and long decking or masonry screws
- Exterior stain and sealer

### MATERIALS TIP

Cedar is often knotty, so choose boards with the fewest and smallest knots that you can find. You may need to throw out some pieces with knots (they will break easily), and you can use some shorter pieces for the horizontals. Also choose relatively clear lumber for the frame.

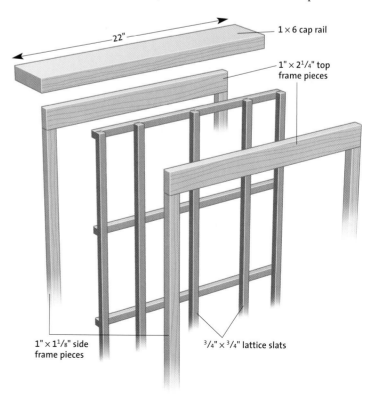

22"

1 × 6 cap rail

1" × 2¹/₄" top frame pieces

1" × 1¹/₈" side frame pieces

³/₄" × ³/₄" lattice slats

**1** **BUILD THE FRAMES.** Rip-cut a ⁵/₄ by 6 to 2¼ inches wide, and cut four pieces to 22 inches (or longer, if you want a wider panel). Rip four more pieces to 1⅛ inches wide, and cut them to the desired height of the panel minus 4½ inches. To assemble each frame, place the pieces on a flat surface, check for square, drill pilot holes, and drive a 4-inch screw into each joint.

**2** **BUILD THE LATTICE.** Rip-cut lattice slats to ¾ inch wide. Cut five verticals to the height of the frame and eight horizontals to the frame's width. Lay the verticals on a flat surface and experiment until you achieve a consistent spacing; cut a scrap board to use as a spacer. Do the same for the horizontals. Check the lattice for square, and fasten each joint by applying a dab of glue and driving a 1¼-inch finish nail or staple.

**3** **SANDWICH FRAMES AND LATTICE.** Place the lattice on top of one frame and lay the second frame over the lattice. Check that the edges are close to flush with each other (the alignment probably won't be perfect), and drive 2½-inch finish nails through the top frame and into the lattice. Turn the assembly over and drive more nails.

**4** **ADD THE CAP RAIL.** Cut a 1 by 6 cap rail to the width of the panel. Position it so it overhangs the panel equally on the front and back, and attach it with 2½-inch nails. Seal and stain after the wood is dry. Attach the panel to the wall using pipe standoffs (see page 35).

# FAN TRELLIS

HERE'S A CLASSIC DESIGN THAT MAKES GOOD SENSE: Like a plant, a fan starts out narrow at the bottom and expands as it rises. It's no wonder this trellis design has been popular for so long. A fan trellis can be secured to a wall or anchored with a stake to stand upright. Or, if there is no danger of wind blowing it over, it can simply be leaned against a house; climbing plants will hold it in place.

## Getting Ready

A custom-made fan trellis is quick and easy to make. The hardest part is rip-cutting the slender slats. A table saw is ideal for this, but you can also use a circular saw equipped with a rip guide (see pages 145–147). Or, have a lumberyard or home center rip the pieces for you.

A power stapler, as shown, makes this work go quickly (see page 150). You can also attach the pieces by drilling pilot holes and driving $1\frac{1}{2}$-inch galvanized nails.

Be sure to use clear lumber; any knots can cause the slats to break easily. Use rot-resistant cedar or treated wood, or coat the pieces with two or three coats of paint.

## Materials List

- One 6' $^5\!/_4 \times 6$ (or 6' 1 × 6) for slats, top piece, and crosspieces
- Two $^1\!/_4$" × $3^1\!/_2$" galvanized carriage bolts with washers and nuts
- Galvanized staples or $1^1\!/_2$" galvanized finish nails
- Exterior wood glue or polyurethane glue
- Exterior primer and paint or stain and sealer
- 3' wood or metal stake (optional)

## BUILDING OPTIONS

Here we show rip-cutting $^5\!/_4$ by 6 decking to $^1\!/_2$ inch thick; for an airier look, rip to $^3\!/_8$-inch-thick slats, and perhaps use 1-by ($^3\!/_4$-inch-thick) lumber.

**1** **RIP THE SLATS.** Use a table saw or circular saw to rip-cut eight $\frac{5}{4}$ by 6 pieces to $\frac{1}{2}$ inch thick. If a piece has a large knot that makes it liable to break, rip another. Apply stain and sealer, or primer and paint, to all the pieces. If the pieces are difficult to bend, place a weight in the middle of the four outermost pieces and wait for a day or so for them to bend.

**2** **BOLT THE BOTTOM.** On a flat surface, put six of the pieces side by side and clamp them together with the bottom ends aligned. Drill two $\frac{1}{4}$-inch holes through the clamped pieces, located 3 inches and 7 inches from the bottom. Take care to drill through the centers of the slats. Tap the bolts through the holes, add washers, and tighten the nuts.

**3** **LAY OUT THE TOP PIECE.** Use a strong, knot-free slat for the top piece. You may want to use a piece that is ripped from the edge of the board; it will have a rounded edge that you can put on top. Cut to 52 inches. Measure and mark lines at 1 inch, 11 inches, 21 inches, 31 inches, 41 inches, and 51 inches, to show where the slats will go.

**4** **ATTACH THE TOP PIECE.** Squirt a dab of glue on top of the first slat, place the outside edge of the top piece against the 1-inch mark, and power-drive a staple. (Or, drill a pilot hole and drive a $1\frac{1}{2}$-inch nail.) Repeat the same process for the rest of the slats, spreading the slats apart as you go.

**5** **ATTACH THE CROSSPIECES.** Cut the last piece into a 40-inch and a 26-inch crosspiece. Lay the crosspieces on top of the trellis so they overhang the slats by about $1\frac{1}{2}$ inches on each side. Fasten them in place with glue and staples or nails. Give the trellis a final coat of sealer or paint. Attach a stake to the rear of the trellis at the bottom using bolts or screws or by wrapping it tightly with wire. Or, simply lean the trellis against the house.

# WIRES ON A WALL

ESPALIER, PRONOUNCED EITHER "ES-PAH-LEE-*ER*" OR "ES-PAH-LEE-*AY*," depending on how French you want to sound, is the art of training plants to grow against a wall in desired shapes. In a formal setting, climbing plants are often made to follow geometric pathways. In an informal backyard, vines may be attached at somewhat more random locations and allowed to follow their natural inclinations in between.

The process can take years, depending on how quickly the plant grows. (Espaliered trees are often managed for decades.) Typically, you will need to spend an hour or so two or three times a year trimming away wayward stems and shoots and encouraging the plant in the directions that please you. The steps opposite show how to provide a structure for a plant trained near a wall, using wire that is stretched taut and held away from the wall by a couple of inches.

## Materials List

- Masonry shields
- Eyehooks sized to fit the shields
- 14-gauge or thicker galvanized wire
- Turnbuckles

## Getting Ready

Consult with a plant expert at a nursery or home center to determine how far away from the wall you should position the wires; thick branches will be trapped by (and may "swallow") wires that are too close. Instead of the 2-inch eyehooks shown here, you may choose to install longer threaded rods with two bolts and run the wire between the bolts.

Steps 1–3 show how to attach eyehooks to a masonry wall, the most typical backdrop for espalier. If your wall is covered with wood or vinyl siding, you can drive eyehooks directly into the wall—as long as the sheathing beneath is solid wood or plywood. Otherwise, drive long eyehooks into the studs instead.

## A Less Formal Espalier

For an organic-looking arrangement like this, allow a plant to grow freely for most of a season. Then prune it to achieve a pleasing shape and position eyehooks or other attachments at critical points. For espalier created this way, you may choose to attach branches to separate eyehooks rather than running wire between eyehooks.

**1** **DRILL HOLES.** For a masonry wall, drill holes using a masonry bit sized for your masonry shields. On some walls, it is easier to drill through brick; on others, mortar. Work slowly and take breaks to avoid overheating the bit and the drill. On tough surfaces, use a hammer drill. Check that the holes are at least ¼ inch deeper than the shield.

**2** **ADD THE SHIELDS.** Use a vacuum (a screw or a piece of wire will also work) to remove most of the dust from the holes. Tap in the shields so they are recessed slightly below the wall surface. If the shields slip in easily and are loose in the hole, tap lightly using a screwdriver or narrow piece of wood to wedge the shield in place.

**3** **SCREW IN EYEHOOKS.** Push against the wall as you screw in the eyehooks, first by hand and then using a screwdriver for more leverage. This causes the shields to expand inside of the holes, making for a tight connection. If a shield starts to pull out, remove the eyehook and shield, drill the hole a bit deeper, and start again.

**4** **STRING THE WIRE.** Wrap the wire twice around the first eyehook, then wrap the end around the wire in a noose-like arrangement. Run the wire from eyehook to eyehook, pulling as taut as possible as you go.

**5** **TIGHTEN WITH A TURNBUCKLE.** Stretch the wire from the end of one run to meet the next wire. Where they meet, use a turnbuckle to make a tight fit. Plan to use a turnbuckle for every three or four turns of the pattern. You may need to retighten the turnbuckles from time to time as the wire stretches slightly.

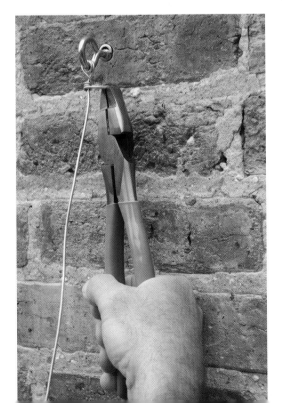

# GARDEN GRID

AS A SINGLE SECTION, THIS UNIT PROVIDES A PLEASING FOCAL POINT. Or, if you build multiple grids, you can combine them to enclose a play area or define a boundary. A fence-like trellis can neatly partition a yard or shield an eyesore like a garbage area, adding more appeal and visual interest than a fence would provide.

## Getting Ready

You could first set the posts in the ground and then build a grid to fit between, but it is usually easier to build the whole structure on a flat surface, then dig postholes and set the posts in the ground. As shown here, the trellis is about 7 feet long and about 4 feet high (including the post caps), with lattice pieces spaced 9 inches apart. You may choose to build a smaller or larger structure, and you may want to space the lattice pieces closer or farther apart.

Use pressure-treated lumber for all the parts; the posts should be rated for ground contact. Depending on how deep your postholes will be, you will probably want to cut the posts to length.

## Materials List

- Two 8' 4 × 4 posts
- One 8' 2 × 4 (or a 2 × 3, if available) for top rail
- Nine 8' 1 × 2s for lattice pieces
- Two post caps
- Short $^5/_4$ by 6 and cove molding (optional)
- $^1/_2$" finish nails and staples, 3" decking or stainless-steel screws
- Exterior wood glue or polyurethane glue
- Exterior wood filler, primer, and paint

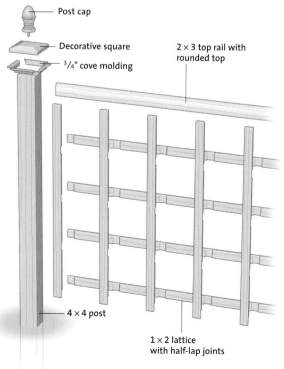

Post cap

Decorative square

$^3/_4$" cove molding

2 × 3 top rail with rounded top

4 × 4 post

1 × 2 lattice with half-lap joints

**1** **BUILD THE LATTICE.** Following the steps shown on pages 152–153, build a lattice grid with lapped joints. Include perimeter pieces only along the sides and the bottom; the top side has no perimeter piece.

**2** **MAKE THE TOP RAIL.** Use a 2 by 3 for your top rail or rip-cut a 2 by 4 to 2¼ inches wide (see pages 145–147). Round off the top edges of the rail using a roundover bit on a router; run the bit on both sides of the edges. Use a power sander or a hand sander to smooth the surfaces (see page 157).

**3** **ATTACH THE GRID.** Set the posts and the grid on a flat surface. Attach the top rail to the posts by drilling angled pilot holes and driving 3-inch screws. Place scrap 1 by 2s under the grid to raise it up so it is centered on the posts and the top rail. Power-drive 2½-inch nails to attach the grid to the posts. To attach it to the top rail, carefully drill long pilot holes and drive 3-inch screws.

**4** **TRIM THE POST TOPS.** For each post top, cut a piece of ⁵⁄₄ by 6 decking to 5½ inches, producing a square. Drill pilot holes and drive screws to attach the squares to the post tops, then drill a pilot hole in the middle of each square and screw in a post cap, also called a newel. If you like, trim the underside of the square piece with cove molding (see page 79). Set the structure in position on the lawn, mark for post-holes, dig the holes, and set the posts in place (see pages 154–155). Once the lumber has dried, apply primer and paint.

## BUILDING OPTIONS

Lattice is usually put together using a power nailer and a power stapler, but you could drill pilot holes and hand-drive galvanized finish nails or drive decking screws. Because the fasteners must be driven through narrow 1 by 2s, take care that the pilot holes are wide enough to prevent cracking.

# GARDEN PANEL

THIS LARGE TRELLIS HAS UNDERSTATED GEOMETRIC LINES that are softened by the look of natural cedar or redwood. The lattice—a grid of 1 by 1s spaced an ample 8 inches apart—has an airy feeling, yet is strong enough to support vigorous and woody climbing plants.

## Getting Ready

This trellis is 90 inches tall and 42 inches wide; the same design could be used for a project that is smaller, or up to 9 feet tall and 5 feet wide. The slats are rip-cut from cedar 1-by lumber with one smooth side and one rough side, which is about $^7/_8$ inch thick. You could also use cedar decking, which is 1 inch thick. If you use cedar fencing, which is about $^5/_8$ inch thick, the trellis will only be strong enough for delicate plants. Of course, you could build with treated lumber instead, and apply stain after the wood has dried.

Rip-cut the lattice slats to $^7/_8$ inch wide (see pages 145–147). Cut seven verticals to the desired height of the lattice and ten horizontals to the desired width. The lattice fits inside the posts, so the structure as a whole will be 7 inches wider than the horizontals. When cutting the verticals, plan so that the lattice will be at least 2 inches above the ground.

### Materials List

- Two 10' 4 × 4 posts
- One 6' 2 × 6 for cap rail
- Two 8' cedar 1 × 6s with one rough side for lattice slats
- $1^1/_4$" and $2^1/_2$" galvanized finish nails or staples
- Exterior wood glue or polyurethane glue
- Gravel
- Exterior stain and sealer

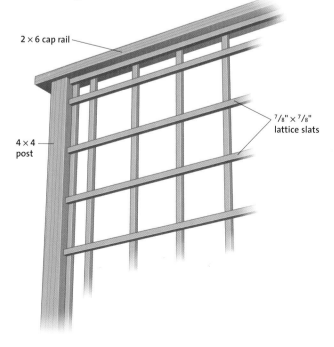

2 × 6 cap rail

$^7/_8$" × $^7/_8$" lattice slats

4 × 4 post

**1** **MAKE THE LATTICE.** Rip the lattice slats from the 1 by 6s. Lay the vertical lattice slats on a flat surface. Apply glue and drive $1\frac{1}{4}$-inch finish nails or staples to attach a horizontal piece to the two outside verticals, then experiment to achieve the desired spacing of the other verticals. Once you have found the magic number, cut a spacer to speed up the process. Do the same for the horizontal slats. If you want the grid to be made of squares, use the same spacer piece as you used for the verticals. The top and bottom horizontals can be positioned differently.

**2** **ATTACH TO THE POSTS.** Allow a few hours for the glue to set, then attach the lattice to the posts. Place a scrap piece of 1-by lumber under the lattice, so it is roughly centered on the posts' thickness, and align the top of the lattice with the top of the posts. Drive $2\frac{1}{2}$-inch finish nails every 6 inches or so.

**3** **ADD THE CAP RAIL.** Cut a 2 by 6 cap rail so it overhangs the posts by 3 inches on each side. Place a 1-by scrap under each post to help center the cap rail over the posts' thickness, and drive $2\frac{1}{2}$-inch finish nails into the posts. Also drive $1\frac{1}{4}$-inch nails up through the lattice and into the cap rail. Set the cedar posts in gravel-filled holes or pound-in post anchors as shown on page 155. Once the wood is dry, seal and stain it.

**PRO TIP**

Partially fill a bucket with sealer/preservative, and set the post bottoms in the bucket. Allow them to soak up the sealer for 15 minutes or so to protect them against rot.

# COPPER TRELLISES

A TRIP THROUGH THE PLUMBING AISLE AT A HOME CENTER yields another cache of potential trellis makings: copper pipe and fittings. With a few basic plumbing tools, you can create any number of trellis designs.

## Working with Copper Pipe

The design shown here uses $\frac{1}{2}$-inch solid copper pipe, which can be bent only slightly; see page 48 for designs that incorporate flexible copper tubing.

Roughly draw up a trellis design and count the number of fittings. You'll likely need tees, 90-degree elbows, 45-degree elbows, and perhaps a cross, which accepts four pipes.

You could solder (or "sweat") the joints (see page 48, or consult Sunset's *Complete Home Plumbing* for more detailed instructions), but you will end up with visible, silver-colored solder at each joint. On these pages, we show applying epoxy glue instead. It's easier for a non-plumbing project, and leaves no visible residue.

If you'll be bending the pipe, use pipe with an "M" rating —it's the least rigid. "L" pipe is stronger, and "K" pipe is the strongest and least bendable.

**1** **CUTTING.** You could cut the pipe using a hacksaw, but a tubing cutter is easier and makes a neater cut. Make any necessary bends in the pipe first. Twist the knob counterclockwise until the pipe can be slipped in between the cutting wheel and the guide wheels. Hold the pipe against the guide wheels and twist the knob clockwise until the blade makes contact and digs in slightly. Next, rotate the cutter a full turn, taking care to keep the tool straight so it forms a single line around the pipe. Tighten again, rotate, and repeat until the pipe snaps in two.

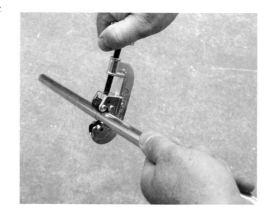

## Materials List

- $\frac{1}{2}$" copper pipe
- $\frac{1}{2}$" copper fittings
- Epoxy glue for attaching metal

### PRO TIP

Left exposed to moisture, copper pipe will turn an attractive blue-green shade (called verdigris) in time. To speed up the greening, brush the pipes with a solution of 3 parts water to one part muriatic acid. If you want the pipes to stay copper-colored, coat them with polyurethane sealer.

**2** **BENDING COPPER PIPE.** You can make gradual curves in copper pipe using an electrician's conduit bender. Place the bender on the floor, slip the pipe in, and pull to make a slight turn. Loosen your grip, move the pipe an inch or so, and repeat. It is usually easier to make the bend first, then cut the pipe to fit.

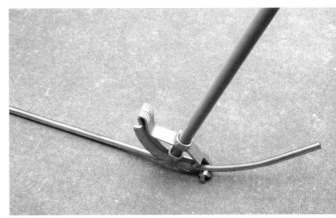

**3** **GLUING.** Cut and dry-fit six or seven pieces to your satisfaction. Disassemble three or four at a time, keeping careful track of which piece goes where. You may occasionally need to mark some fittings and pipes to show the exact direction they should face. The epoxy adhesive shown here requires mixing two components together just prior to attaching; it sets up in 5 minutes or so. Rub the pipe ends and the insides of the fittings with 100-grit sandpaper or plumber's emery cloth until the metal shines and is lightly roughed up. Mix the epoxy, apply it to the pipe end or the inside of the fitting, and push the pieces together. Assemble the parts quickly, then allow the epoxy to set before moving on to the next group of joints.

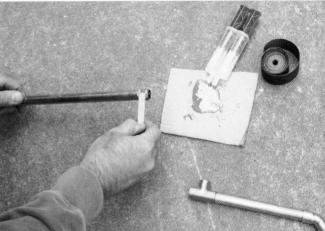

## Pipes in a Pot

This narrow copper trellis slides easily into a flower pot, adding a gleaming accent. Left unfinished, it will turn a mellow green that blends with climbing stems and tendrils.

If you do not find ³/₈-inch copper pipe (which has an outside diameter of ¹/₂ inch) and fittings at a home center, look for them at a plumbing supply store.

On a small project like this, any variations in pipe lengths will be noticeable, so mark the pipes precisely for cutting and position the cutting wheel right on the marks. If two mirroring pieces are not the same size, throw one out and try again.

Cut and dry-assemble all the pieces, then stand back to inspect the arrangement. Disassemble only two or three pieces at a time, and fasten with epoxy as shown above. Or, fasten by soldering the joints (see page 48).

Once it's finished, simply poke the trellis into the pot's soil.

### Materials List

- ³/₈" copper pipe
- ³/₈" copper fittings, including 90° and 45° elbows, tees
- Epoxy glue for attaching metal

## Materials List

- ½" copper pipe
- ½" copper fittings, including 90°
  and 45° elbows, tees, cross (optional)
- ½" or ⅜" flexible copper tubing
- Epoxy glue for attaching metal
- Solder and flux

## Scrolled Screen

An ornate copper-pipe trellis like this is both stunning and quaint at the same time. With so many curves, it may appear out of your skill range, but building it calls for patience and care rather than special skills. Aim for smooth curves and symmetrical designs, but perfection is not expected.

You will join the curved tubing to the pipes using solder, which means that you will end up with rough-looking silver-colored joints. To maintain a consistent rustic look, you may want to attach the pipes and fittings with solder as well. For the very curved pieces, use ½-inch flexible copper tubing, or, for a more delicate look, ⅜-inch tubing.

- **FIRST BUILD A PIPE TRELLIS,** as shown on pages 46–47. The trellis shown at left has gently curved pieces that meet at a 90-degree elbow fitting at the top. Once the basic trellis is built, fill in with the heavily curved tubing. To approach symmetry, cut and bend one section, test its fit, then use it as a template for making mirroring sections.

- **BEND THE COPPER TUBING.**
Tubing bends easily, but if you try to bend it by hand you will find it difficult to avoid kinking—and a kink cannot be straightened out.

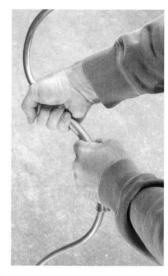

A simple spring-like tubing bending tool makes it easy to produce smooth, kink-free curves.

- **SOLDER THE CONNECTIONS.** It takes a bit of a knack to produce firm soldered joints with minimal mess, so practice on scrap pieces before attempting the real thing. Rub the pieces with emery cloth or sandpaper until the copper turns a bright color and is roughed up. Spread an ample amount of flux onto both pieces. To keep the pieces still while you work, have a helper (with gloved hands—the pipes get very hot) hold the tubing against a pipe, use clamps, or lay the pieces on a flat surface with a protective heat shield under the joint.

- **WITH THE PIECES HELD TOGETHER,** fire up a propane torch and touch the tip of the flame to the pipe on one side of the joint, then the other. (Do not apply flame to the joint itself.) Touch the end of the solder to the joint. Once the liquid solder sucks into the joint, stop heating and gently wipe off the excess with a damp rag as needed. If the joint is not firm when the solder cools, disassemble and try again.

# TWO WAYS WITH REBAR

CONCRETE REINFORCING BAR, aka rebar, can be used to create straight or curved lines that are surprisingly stylish. Rebar comes in $\frac{1}{2}$- and $\frac{3}{8}$-inch thicknesses. Avoid the green painted stuff; you want bare metal.

## Arched

The most difficult part of this project is getting 20-foot lengths of $\frac{1}{2}$-inch rebar to the site. Choose pieces that are free of bends. If possible, have them delivered by the supplier. Otherwise, tie the pieces tightly together with pieces of wire or duct tape. Tie them to a board that is at least 12 feet long to keep them from rolling and sliding while you drive.

Installing is a fun two-person job. Wear gloves, or expect to spend time washing away ground-in rust. Stand the rebar up and poke it at least 16 inches into the ground. Have one person hold the first end firm while the other bends it over and pokes it into the ground. If you accidentally produce a sharp bend, you can usually straighten it out.

## Straight Up

Vertical, evenly spaced pieces of rebar make for an unusual and handsome trellis. This project looks even simpler than the one above, but it actually takes a bit more time and care to keep the pieces straight, parallel, and evenly spaced. The design at right uses 10-foot pieces of $\frac{1}{2}$-inch rebar.

Take care to buy rebar pieces that are straight. Poke the pieces straight into the ground, using a scrap of lumber as a spacer tool. Use a hacksaw or a reciprocating saw equipped with a metal-cutting blade to cut a horizontal piece of rebar to the desired width of the trellis. Place the cut rebar piece on the ground next to the trellis and mark it with a crayon for the positions of the vertical pieces. Working with a helper, place the cut rebar behind the verticals and carefully attach the verticals with wire made for use with rebar or 14-gauge copper wire, using lineman's pliers to twist the wires for tight joints.

# BENTWOOD TRELLISES

A RUSTIC TRELLIS MADE OF BRANCHES CAN BE A FOCAL POINT IF IT IS LARGE AND EXPOSED, or it may be barely noticeable once vines climb over it. Bentwood trellises like these are a venerable tradition in many parts of the country. Making one requires no special skills, but it helps to have patience and a critical eye. A small amount of artistic talent will go a long way.

## Getting Ready

You may spend more time scrounging materials than you spend making the trellis. Here we use willow, whose new tendrils have a string-like flexibility. In general, newly cut branches of almost any tree will be at least somewhat flexible. If possible, build the trellis the same day the branches are cut. Soaking newly cut branches in water does not increase or prolong their flexibility.

To find branches, see if your municipality has crews of tree cutters; you may be able to tag along and pull out branches before they are run through a chipper. Or check a local nursery or woody areas. Trees that grow near a swamp, pond, or river often have good flexibility. Cedar, cypress, oak, elm, and apple will likely last for at least a few years. Scrubby or fast-growing trees like sycamore, mulberry, and grapevines may rot within a year.

## Materials List

- A good supply (twice as much as you think you need) of freshly cut, flexible branches or saplings in a variety of thicknesses
- Copper wire
- Decking screws, various lengths, in a color that blends with the branches

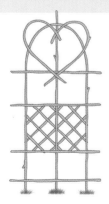
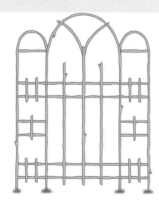
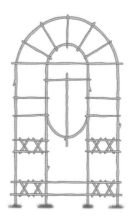

SAMPLE BENTWOOD DESIGNS

**1** **CHOOSE AND STRIP THE BRANCHES.**
Choose fairly straight branches of roughly the same thickness for members that mirror each other. Remove most of the leaves and small branches that will not be a part of the trellis. A hand pruner will handle most of the cutting.

**2** **CUT WITH A SAW.**
Place mirroring pieces on a flat surface and cut them to the same size, both in length and thickness. (In this design, the top portions of the outer uprights will bend and cross at the top.) Use a small handsaw or a reciprocating saw to cut thicker branches.

**3** **CHOOSE AND CUT CROSSPIECES.** Use straight branches that are a bit thinner than the uprights for crosspieces. Cut them so they have consistent overhangs. It may look best to have crosspieces that are progressively thinner as they ascend.

**4** **ATTACH WITH SCREWS.** You could learn to attach branches using willow or other flexible branches, but most of us need to use more modern methods. Decking screws can be driven into the wood so the heads are nearly buried. If the screw pokes out the back, bend the excess back and forth with pliers until it breaks.

**5** **LOOP THE TOP.** Bend the thin upper portions of the uprights and twist them together so they are secure. Stand back and cast a critical eye over the structure, then adjust the loop until you achieve a look that pleases you.

**6** **ATTACH THINNER PIECES WITH WIRE.** The heart shape of this trellis is made with two thin branches that cannot be screwed. Starting at the thickest parts of the branches, place the pieces in position (you can cut them to length later) and twist wire around them, first by hand and then using lineman's pliers. With a bit of care you can produce a neat twist. You may choose to cover the wired joint with twisted tendrils.

**7** **MAKE A DECORATIVE SHAPE.** Loop the thin branches to form a heart or another shape, then attach them with wire. Hold the trellis upright; loosen the wire and adjust the branches as needed, then retighten. Finally, cut the loose ends evenly.

## Rustic Screen

A branchy trellis doesn't have to be a small endeavor. For large spaces, build a trellis on a scale to match the environment, like the one at right. In technique and materials, this falls midway between the bentwood trellis shown above and the rough-hewn arbor on pages 114–117. You'll need freshly cut branches or saplings 3 to 4 inches in diameter; flexible branches about 1 inch in diameter; decking screws of various lengths in a color that blends with the branches; long spikes (see page 117); and copper wire.

To join the major pieces, notch the uprights and cut the ends of the crosspieces as shown on page 115. Use long screws or spikes to make the connections. Screw the smaller pieces in place. The uprights can be spiked to the ground or secured to rebar stakes.

# TWO WAYS WITH BAMBOO

BAMBOO IS GENERALLY STRAIGHT, but with interesting natural variations in shape and node placement. This makes it an ideal material for trellises or for portions of an arbor.

## As a Fence

The trellis shown below uses bamboo stalks that are all the same thickness. You may prefer to use large-diameter pieces for main supports and smaller diameters for the other pieces.

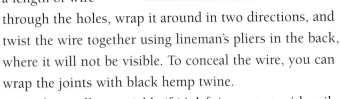

### Materials List

- Bamboo (available in ½" to 4" diameters and lengths up to 12')
- Copper or galvanized steel wire
- 3' lengths of ⅜" rebar

Drill through the stalks where they intersect. Feed a length of wire through the holes, wrap it around in two directions, and twist the wire together using lineman's pliers in the back, where it will not be visible. To conceal the wire, you can wrap the joints with black hemp twine.

Bamboo will rot quickly if it's left in contact with soil. To make it last longer, slip the pieces over 3-foot lengths of ⅜-inch rebar driven into the ground. You may need to use a long ½-inch drill bit to drill through nodes on the inside of the bamboo near the bottom.

## In a Pot

Here's a cute little guy you can assemble in a few minutes. At a home center or nursery, look for bamboo bent in a U shape. Poke these pieces, crisscrossed, into a pot or the ground, or keep them off the ground with the rebar technique described above. For an extra flourish, tie decorative grass at the top. This trellis is loosely wrapped with a light plastic mesh, offering more support to the climbing plant.

# TEPEES

FOR A QUICK, INEXPENSIVE SUPPORT FOR CLIMBING PLANTS, try building a tepee. Because they are easily moved, tepees lend themselves to vegetables such as runner beans, which may not occupy the same spot next year. Growing vegetables on a tepee is fun for children, too. Not only does the structure put the veggies at a convenient height for harvesting, but the foliage creates a hideaway under the poles.

Depending on the wood species you choose for the poles (see page 50), a tepee may last only a year or two, or it could stay rot-free for six or seven years. For a longer-lasting tepee, wrap with copper or galvanized steel wire, then cover the wire with a rope made of grapevines or willow; you may need to replace the wrapping every year or so.

You can make a simple pole tepee by arranging the poles, poking them in the ground, and wrapping with wire at the top. The version shown here has additional garlands made of willow.

**1** **MAKE A BRANCH ROPE.** If you use fairly thick grapevines as shown at left, first build the tepee, wrapped with wire at the top, then weave the vines in and out of the poles at various heights.

When using thinner materials like the thin ends of willow branches, form them into a rope by plaiting them together. Overlap the pieces and twist them together. Then wrap more tightly with slender pieces that form tight loops.

## Materials List

- Three to six poles, 1½" to 2½" in diameter and 4' to 7' long
- Copper or galvanized steel wire
- Grapevines or flexible willow branches

**2** **FORM THE TEPEE AND WRAP THE TOP.** Arrange the poles so they splay out at regular intervals. You may choose to tie the top using only the branches, or you can wrap first with wire, then cover the wire with a branch rope.

**3** **ADD GARLANDS.** For each garland, loosely tie a branch rope around the poles. Then wrap individual thin branches to tie the rope to each of the poles.

## Used-Tool Tepee

Those old tools you have lying around in the garage may be too weathered to be of practical use, but consider forming them into a rustic tepee. Once placed in a garden setting, all that rusty metal and weather-beaten wood becomes charming and nostalgia-inducing.

This tepee starts with a common galvanized steel tomato cage, cut to fit. This takes the bulk of the foliage, allowing the used tools to be on greater display. The garden tools are simply placed outside the tomato support and tied at the top with twine. Most old tools have handles made of hickory or other very hard wood, so they can last for a surprising number of years before starting to rot.

# A VERTICAL HARVEST

MANY VEGETABLES AND FRUITS (LIKE THE RASPBERRY BUSH SHOWN HERE) benefit from the support and elevation of a trellis. Pages 58–59 include some simpler trellises that are also well suited to the purpose. This one takes more time to build, but adds a touch of elegance to a garden patch.

## Getting Ready

Use your gardening experience or consult with a plant expert at a nursery to determine the best height and spacing for the posts. A raspberry bush easily grows to 5 feet tall or more; other plants may benefit from a shorter structure. Here we show a trellis with two crosspieces, but you may decide to use three or more.

Use pressure-treated lumber; the posts should be rated for ground contact. Set the posts in postholes, or attach them to stakes driven into the ground so you can move them later.

## Materials List

- Two 8' 4 × 4 posts with finials
- One 8' 2 × 10 for four crosspieces
- Eight $1/4$" × 5" galvanized carriage bolts with washers and nuts
- Sixteen $1/4$" × 4" rust-resistant eyebolts with 32 washers and 32 nuts
- Exterior primer and paint
- 14-gauge or thicker galvanized wire

## PRO TIP

If possible, build with wood that is already dry, so you can paint the pieces before assembly. If the wood is wet, build early in the spring, so you can allow it to dry for a few weeks before painting. You may want to wait until after you paint to install the eyebolts and wire.

**1** **CUT THE CROSSPIECES.** Sketch shapes for an upper and a lower crosspiece on a piece of plywood or cardboard; the exact curves aren't important as long as you like them. Trace two of each on the 2 by 10, fitting the two longer pieces end to end and nestling the other two in the remaining areas. Set the board on sawhorses and cut the pieces with a jigsaw.

**2** **NOTCH THE POSTS FOR THE CROSS-PIECES.** Mark for the top of the upper crosspiece notch about 1 inch below the finial cut, and for the top of the lower crosspiece notch 8 inches below the bottom of the upper one. With your circular saw set to a 3/4-inch depth, make numerous cuts through each marked notch area, then clean out the notch with a chisel.

**3** **ATTACH THE CROSSPIECES.** If the treated wood is dry, prime and paint the posts and crosspieces. Seat the crosspieces in the notches. Drill two 1/4-inch holes through each crosspiece and as far as possible into the post; set the crosspieces aside to extend the holes all the way through the posts. Attach the crosspieces to the posts with carriage bolts.

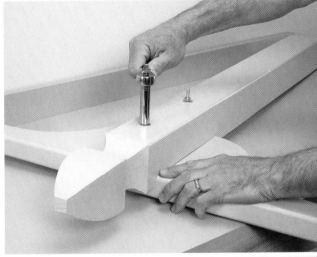

**4** **STRING THE GUIDE WIRES.** Drill 1/4-inch holes for the eyebolts near both ends of each upper crosspiece and also about 6 inches out from the posts. Thread nuts and washers on the eyebolts, push them through the holes, and lock them in place with more washers and nuts. Add eyebolts to the lower crosspieces as well. Dig postholes 2 or 3 feet deep (see page 154) and set the posts in place, checking for plumb as you tamp down the soil. String the galvanized wire between the crosspieces, feeding it through an eyebolt twice and twisting it with pliers, then running it to the corresponding eye on the opposite post (it doesn't have to be taut) and securing it the same way.

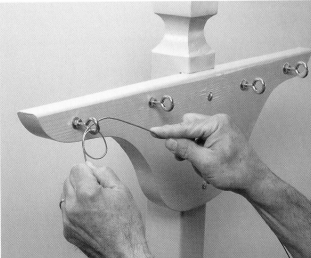

# MORE VEGGIE TRELLISES

## Pole-and-Mesh Vegetable Trellises

Vegetable trellises are all too often flimsy, awkward-looking structures. But it's not hard to build a trellis that is handsome and will last a decade or more. A farm store may be your best source for materials for this modest yet sturdy structure.

• **CUT THE HORIZONTAL RAILS 4 OR 5 FEET LONG.** Lay the posts and rails on the ground to determine the positions for the postholes; if there will be more than two posts, use a string to make sure they form a straight line. Dig the holes at least 2 feet deep.

• **SET THE FIRST POST IN ITS HOLE** and check for plumb as you tamp the soil around it. Set the second post, checking that it is at the same height as the first post; you may need to make the hole deeper or fill it in slightly, tamping well. Drill pilot holes through the posts, one near the top and one about a foot above the ground. Have a helper hold the rails in place while you drive lag screws to fasten the rails to the posts. Drive the screw heads fairly deep into the posts. Firmly tamp the ground around all the posts.

• **HAVE ONE OR TWO HELPERS HOLD THE WIRE MESH** as you staple it to the first post, taking care to make the mesh parallel to the rails. As your helper or helpers carefully unroll the mesh, pull it taut and continue to staple it to the rails and posts. Cut the leftover mesh using wire cutters or lineman's pliers.

## Materials List

- Cedar or pine poles, 3" to 4" diameter
- Roll of galvanized cattle fencing or pig wire
- $1/4$" by 7" lag screws
- 2" fencing staples, or staples for a power-drive gun
- Exterior stain and sealer

## PRO TIP

If you want the bottom rail to align with a horizontal strand of the wire mesh, measure the mesh and plan the rail's exact height.

## Crisscross Rustic Trellis

A rustic trellis like this approaches elegance if it is constructed carefully, with branches that are fairly consistent in thickness and evenly spaced. Choose branches that are straight and that have firmly attached bark.

● DIG POSTHOLES AND INSTALL THICK BRANCHES or 4 by 4 posts at either end of the trellis, or spaced at least every 6 feet if the trellis is longer than 8 feet. Check that the posts are roughly the same height. If you have more than two, stretch a string between the first and last post to ensure the others are in a straight line.

● PLACE THE LONG TOP RAIL ON TOP OF THE POSTS and drive nails or screws to attach it. With a tape measure and pencil, mark the rail every 12 inches or so for the positions of the uprights.

● STARTING IN THE MIDDLE, set one end of an angled upright branch on the ground and nail the other end to the top rail. It's fine if the uprights are too long; you can cut them later. Use a spacer to maintain a fairly consistent angle as you add the other uprights, all facing the same direction. Then add the uprights that face the other way.

### Materials List

- Straight branches for top rail, and shorter branches (about 4') for angled uprights
- Two thick branches or 4 × 4s for posts
- Power-driven nails or decking or stainless-steel screws, long enough to penetrate most of the way through two branches

## Veggie Panel with a Point

If you are like many vegetable gardeners, you probably rotate your crops to avoid disease and to rest the soil. Here's a lightweight trellis you can move easily as the need arises.

● SCREW HORIZONTAL PIECES TO THE OUTSIDE VERTICALS, alternating them from one face to the other. Leave about 12 inches of the verticals to sink into the ground.

● CUT ANGLES ON THE ENDS OF THE DIAGONAL PIECES to fit against the center vertical. Weave the diagonal pieces and the center vertical through the horizontal pieces. Screw them to the horizontals, so the trellis does not rack, and then screw the diagonals to the center vertical near the top.

● TIE THE NYLON STRINGS IN PLACE. Then cap the structure with a fun ornament like the copper fish at left.

### Materials List

- 1 × 2s
- Nylon string
- 1¼" decking screws

# PLANTER TRELLIS

DON'T LET THE LACK OF A LARGE OPEN SPACE LIMIT YOUR GARDEN ASPIRATIONS. Container gardening opens up a world of possibilities, particularly when the container is paired with a built-in trellis.

## Getting Ready

This planter box is built of inexpensive cedar fencing, which is typically about ⅝ inch thick and rough on each side. Use it as a housing for potted plants, or build it to fit around a plastic planter box or two; it's not strong or rot-resistant enough to be directly filled with soil. If you want to fill the box with soil, use ⁵⁄₄ by 6s instead of fencing and coat the inside with plenty of sealer. The box and the lattice can be stained and sealed, or can be left to turn a rustic gray in a year or two. Be sure to use treated plywood and 2 by 2s.

If you plan to move the planter often, screw casters (wheels) to the bottom at the corners. If you will move it only occasionally, it will not be difficult to pick it up with a helper.

### Materials List

- Eleven 6' cedar fencing boards for box and lattice
- Four 8' 2 × 2s for interior framing
- Half a sheet of ³⁄₄" plywood for bottom shelf
- 2½" galvanized finish nails or decking or stainless-steel screws; 1" staples or finish nails
- Exterior wood glue or polyurethane glue
- Exterior stain and sealer

### PRO TIP

Once plants start growing onto a trellis, it will be difficult, if not impossible, to repaint or restain it without damaging the climbing plants. So take the time now to apply a thick protective coating.

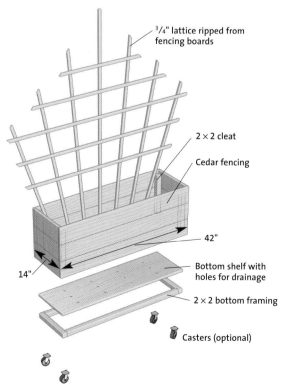

³⁄₄" lattice ripped from fencing boards

2 × 2 cleat

Cedar fencing

42"

14"

Bottom shelf with holes for drainage

2 × 2 bottom framing

Casters (optional)

**1** **ASSEMBLE THREE BOX RECTANGLES.** Cut six 42-inch and six 14-inch pieces from the fencing boards. Form three rectangles. Drive two finish nails or screws into each corner. The boxes will not be rigid at this point.

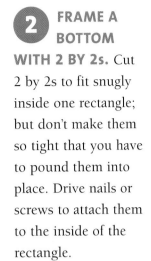

**2** **FRAME A BOTTOM WITH 2 BY 2s.** Cut 2 by 2s to fit snugly inside one rectangle; but don't make them so tight that you have to pound them into place. Drive nails or screws to attach them to the inside of the rectangle.

**3** **MAKE THE BOTTOM SHELF.** Measure the inside dimensions of the rectangle and cut a piece of treated plywood to fit; this will be the bottom shelf. Drill a grid of 1/4-inch holes in the shelf for drainage.

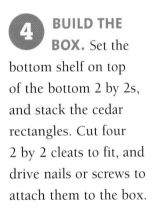

**4** **BUILD THE BOX.** Set the bottom shelf on top of the bottom 2 by 2s, and stack the cedar rectangles. Cut four 2 by 2 cleats to fit, and drive nails or screws to attach them to the box.

**5** **MAKE THE LATTICE.** Rip-cut ten or eleven 3/4-inch-wide lattice slats (see pages 146–147). Unless you have perfectly clear lumber, some of the pieces will break at knots; use these for the shorter slats. Install a 6-foot slat in the center as the middle upright, checking that it is square to the box. Arrange and cut the other slats until you achieve a pattern that pleases you. Attach the slats to the box and the other lattice slats with dollops of glue and 1-inch staples. Or, carefully drill pilot holes from behind and drive 1-inch screws.

# RAISED-BED TRELLIS

A LARGE RAISED BED LIKE THIS PROVIDES AMPLE SPACE FOR MANY TYPES OF GARDENING PROJECTS. Unlike a planter, a raised bed has no bottom and is a permanent structure. The lattice panel allows vines to climb in back; if the unit faces south, the climbing plants will not shade the plants in front. The planter is at a comfortable height, so you do not have to kneel down when planting and weeding. The planter's top cap provides a pleasant place to sit.

## Getting Ready

This is a heavy-duty project that uses substantial lumber pieces. Choose pressure-treated pieces that are straight and free of serious defects. The posts are sunk in the ground, so they should be rated for ground contact. The bottom 2 by 6s rest on the ground and the inside will be filled with soil, so either buy ground-contact lumber or, if that is not available, apply a generous coat of sealer to the inside and bottom of the box.

Choose a fairly flat and level spot, or dig away high spots. Because the planter is so deep, you do not need to excavate away sod at the bottom; few roots from your plants will reach that deep. This planter is about 7 feet by 4 feet, but you can change the size. If your planter is longer than 8 feet, it should have two interior dividers.

## Materials List

- Two 8' 4 × 4 posts
- One 8' 2 × 8 for front cap
- Sixteen 8' 2 × 6s for box framing and corner trim
- Four 8' 2 × 4s for cap rail, blocks, and side caps
- Two 8' 2 × 2s for cleats
- Four 8' 1 × 2s for lattice frame
- Two sheets of heavy-duty (³/₄" thick) treated lattice
- 3" decking or stainless-steel screws, 3" galvanized nails, 2¹/₂" galvanized finish nails
- Exterior stain and sealer

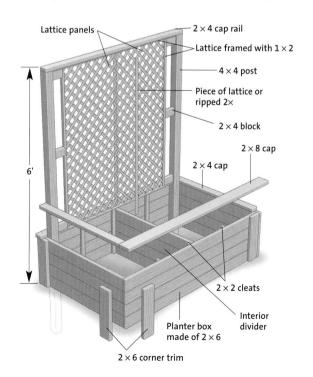

Lattice panels

2 × 4 cap rail

Lattice framed with 1 × 2

4 × 4 post

Piece of lattice or ripped 2×

2 × 4 block

2 × 8 cap

2 × 4 cap

6'

2 × 2 cleats

Interior divider

Planter box made of 2 × 6

2 × 6 corner trim

**1** **LEVEL AND SQUARE THE FIRST COURSE.** For the planter box, cut twelve 2 by 6s to get eight 7-foot pieces and eight 46-inch pieces. Assemble the first course (the bottom rectangle), driving two power nails or drilling pilot holes and driving two screws at each joint. Set the course on the ground at the planned location and check that it is fairly level, digging away remaining high spots if necessary. Check that the box is square by making sure the diagonals are the same length. (You can also use a piece of plywood with factory edges.)

**2** **DIG POSTHOLES AND BUILD THE BOX.** Dig postholes at the two back corners. Make them at least 2 feet deep. Set the posts in the holes. Build the remaining three box courses, stacking them on top of each other and around the posts as you go. As you work, continually check the box and the posts for plumb in both directions (see pages 154–155). Drive screws or nails through the 2 by 6s and into the posts.

**3** **INSTALL CORNER TRIM.** Cut eight 2 by 6 pieces to the height of the box, minus half an inch or so to keep the cut ends off the ground. Working on a flat surface, assemble the pieces into corner trim by driving three nails or drilling pilot holes and driving three screws. Attach the trim assemblies to the corners, making sure the tops are flush with the top of the box.

**4** **ADD THE INSIDE FRAMING.** To keep the 2 by 6s from bellying out when the planter is filled with soil, build an interior dividing wall. Attach 2 by 2 cleats to the insides of the box, then fit and attach four courses of 2 by 6s between the 2 by 2s. Also install four additional cleats, positioned midway between the corners and the interior dividing wall.

**5** **CAP THE BOX.** Cut a 2 by 8 so it overhangs each side of the box by 3 inches. Center it over the front board, and drive nails or screws to attach it. To cap the remaining three sides, carefully measure and cut 2 by 4s so they wrap tightly around the posts and attach in the same way. Cut both posts to the same height above the box.

**6** **CUT THE TRELLIS PARTS.** For the trellis, cut two 1 by 2s to span between the posts (one for the bottom and one for the top). Cut two more to the height of the trellis—from the top of the box to the top of the posts. Now comes the trickier part: Cut two lattice panels to the same height as the side 1 by 2s; make them half the width of the top and bottom 1 by 2s, minus 3½ inches. Plan the cuts carefully, so the trellis patterns match up fairly closely. (Because of the way the panels are made, it will probably not be possible to match the patterns exactly.) Lay the parts out on a flat surface, so you can check the fits and the pattern match as you work.

**BUILDING** OPTIONS

The trellis is assembled by attaching directly to a modest 1 by 2 frame, with none of the usual "sandwiching" pieces. This calls for some accurate nailing, so you may want to practice on scrap pieces before attempting the real thing. If you are uncomfortable with this technique, make the frame out of 2 by 4s instead of 1 by 2s, and use sandwiching 1 by 2s as shown, for example, on page 89.

**7** **START NAILING THE TRELLIS TOGETHER.** To cover the seam between the two trellis panels, use leftover trellis pieces, or rip-cut pieces of 2-by to ⅜ inch. Position the panels so they are centered on the top and bottom 1 by 2s. Power-drive finish nails through the 1 by 2s and into the panels. This calls for accurate nailing, so practice on scrap pieces before nailing the real thing.

**8** **FINISH ASSEMBLING THE TRELLIS FRAME.** Complete the frame by nailing the 1 by 2s together at the corners.

**9** **ATTACH THE CAP RAIL AND TRELLIS.** Cut a 2 by 4 as a cap rail to span over the tops of the posts, and attach with nails or screws. Position the trellis assembly between the posts, and drive nails to attach it to the cap rail.

**10** **ADD THE SIDE BLOCKS.** Cut 2 by 4 blocks to fit between the grid and the posts on either side. Drill angled pilot holes and drive screws to attach the blocks to the posts; drive finish nails through the trellis frame and into the side blocks.

**11** **FINISH WITH TRIM.** A tasteful touch like the trim piece shown here takes little time and greatly enhances the appearance of the structure. This one was cut from a 2 by 6; a roundover bit on a router made the decorative edges (see page 157). Once the structure's wood has dried, apply stain and sealer.

# OBELISK

A GARDEN TOWER WITH THE CRISP GEOMETRY OF AN OBELISK adds a stunning focal point and a vertical dimension to your garden. Once vines climb onto the obelisk, the contrast between natural and constructed elements will enhance the appeal. This obelisk is made from pressure-treated lumber, left to weather naturally.

## Getting Ready

Building the obelisk isn't that difficult if you have good tools and basic carpentry skills. There are some tricky angled cuts, though, that you'll need to make to get the legs to splay correctly. The good thing is that even if you are off a little bit, the tower will still work. Because the legs are long, you can flex them slightly to get everything to line up.

Start with a post top with a pointy finial. To rip-cut the lath pieces, see page 146. These photos show attaching with screws, but you can also use power-driven finish nails and staples; don't attempt to hand-nail. You can apply exterior wood glue or polyurethane glue to the joints for added strength.

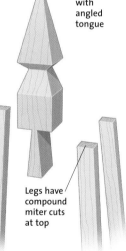

Post top with angled tongue

Legs have compound miter cuts at top

## Materials List

- One 4 × 4 fence post with finial, cut about 14" long
- Four 8' 2 × 2s for 93½" legs
- One 8' 2 × 4 for four 22" spreaders
- Four 4' pieces of ¼" × 1½" lath, perhaps rip-cut from a 2 × 4, for: four 17½" lower crosspieces, four 14" middle crosspieces, and four 10½" upper crosspieces
- Four 7' pieces of ¼" × 1" lath, perhaps rip-cut from ⁵/₄ decking, for four long verticals
- Eight 5' pieces of ¼" × 1" lath for eight shorter verticals
- 1¼" and 2" decking or stainless-steel screws

PRO TIP

Especially when you are working with ¼-inch lath, which splits easily, countersink your pilot holes (see page 151). Countersinking helps keep the wood from splitting, and also ensures the screw heads will sit flush with the surface for a neater appearance.

**1** **CUT THE TONGUE.** Mark the cut post top for a tongue. The tongue should be 3⅜ inches long and wider at its base than at its shoulders. Make it 1 inch wide at the base, tapering to ½ inch at the shoulders. Set a circular saw to make a cut 1½ inches deep, and cut the line at the top of the shoulder. Then set the saw to full depth and cut the other (tapered) line, taking care not to cut too far. Flip the post over and cut from the other side, then finish the cut using a handsaw. Cut the other side of the tongue in the same way.

**2** **ATTACH THE LEGS.** The tops of the legs are cut on a compound angle—that is, the saw blade is set at an angle, and it runs across the piece at an angle as well. (See the illustration at left.) The magic number is 6 degrees. Make the cuts 6 degrees off square (that is, either 96 degrees or 84 degrees, depending on how you hold the square) with the blade also tilted 6 degrees. Position the legs against the post tongue and test to see that the leg bottoms are fairly close to 22 inches apart; adjust the angles if needed. Drill pilot holes and attach the legs to the post top with 2-inch screws.

**3** **INSTALL THE SPREADERS.** Cut the spreaders to length, angling the ends at 6 degrees off square so they will follow the lines of the spread-apart legs. Position the spreaders about 10 inches above the bottom of the legs. Drill pilot holes and screw the spreaders to the legs. You may need to flex the legs a little to make the spreaders fit.

**4** **ATTACH THE INNER PIECES.** Cut the crosspieces, angling the ends at 6 degrees off square. Space them 15 inches apart on the legs, starting from the top of the spreaders. Drill countersunk pilot holes (see page 151) and screw the crosspieces to the legs with 1¼-inch screws. Weave the verticals over and under the crosspieces. Fasten the verticals to the post and the spreaders with 1¼-inch screws.

# TRELLISED FENCE

A FENCE WITH CLOSED-SPACED LATTICE OFFERS PRIVACY— or a good way to hide those unappealing garbage cans— while maintaining an airy feel. Plants can climb onto this fence, though only the thinnest of tendrils will be able to interweave between the lattice slats.

## Getting Ready

You may need to hunt around to find suitable posts. Here we show rough-cut pressure-treated 6 by 6 posts, which are available at some lumberyards. They are actually 6 inches by 6 inches (standard 6 by 6s are $5\frac{1}{2}$ inches square) with a rough surface. You could simply use treated 6 by 6s, but the surface will be smooth. Treated timbers tend to have cracks; choose the posts carefully, so at least one side (where the grooves will go) is nearly crack-free.

You could also opt for rough-cut 6 by 6 cedar posts, which generally have fewer cracks. However, these tend to cost three to four times as much as treated posts. Another option is to buy posts that are already decorated with grooves. These are available from specialty fencing sources; a lumberyard may be able to order them for you. Again, the price will be higher.

Because you must rout the grooves before setting the posts in the ground, you cannot cut the posts to height after they are set. That means you will need to adjust posthole depths in order to maintain a consistent post height.

## Materials List

- 8' rough-cut treated 6 × 6 posts as needed
- 2 × 6s for ripping lattice slats and nailers
- 1 × 4s for cap rails and top rails
- Post caps
- 3" framing nails; 2" finish nails; ³/₄" finish nails or staples
- Exterior primer and paint or sealer and stain

## PRO TIP

If the fence is on a slope, you may need to step the posts up or down to suit the terrain. Keep the lattice sections level—meaning that the lattice will be lower on one side of a post and higher on the other—rather than trying to angle the lattice. For general information on fence building, see Sunset's *Fences, Walls & Gates*.

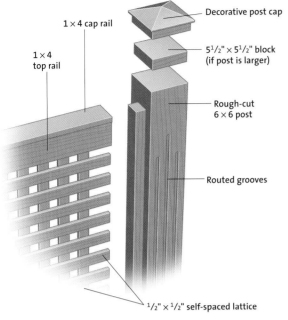

1 × 4 cap rail

Decorative post cap

1 × 4 top rail

5¹/₂" × 5¹/₂" block (if post is larger)

Rough-cut 6 × 6 post

Routed grooves

¹/₂" × ¹/₂" self-spaced lattice

**1** **MEASURE AND CUT POSTS.** The fence shown here is 5 feet tall, but it can easily be made higher or lower. You will probably need to cut off some cracked posts at the top, for appearance's sake. These cuts need to be fairly precise. Use a square to carefully draw lines all around the post; if they do not meet at the end, move down half an inch and try again. Check your circular saw to make sure the blade is square to the base plate (see page 145) and cut all four lines.

**2** **FINISH THE CUT.** The circular saw will not cut all the way through. Finish cutting the posts using a handsaw or a reciprocating saw.

**3** **CUT THE LATTICE.** This design uses plenty of lattice slats, so expect to spend some time with your table saw or circular saw equipped with a rip guide (see pages 145–147). Rip-cut ¹/₂-inch-thick slats from the 2 by 6s.

**4** **CHOOSE YOUR GROOVES.** Plan and mark for the desired grooves. In this project, we use a ¹/₂-inch-wide router bit to cut three grooves, with the centers of the outer grooves 1¹/₂ inches from the post edges. You can also use the techniques in Steps 5 and 6 to cut sample grooves in a scrap piece (or the portion of a post that will be sunk in the ground) and adjust the design to suit your tastes.

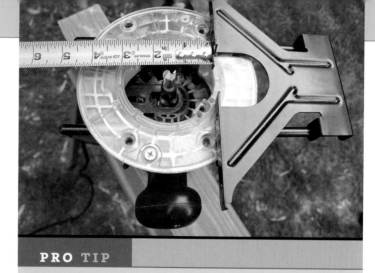

**5** **SET UP FOR ROUTING.** Set a ½-inch router bit to cut about ⅜ inch deep. Slide a rip guide onto the router, and adjust it for the first groove. Measure from the rip guide to the center of the router bit to find the center of the groove.

**PRO TIP**

Routing grooves is not difficult, but it is easy to slip up and create a wandering line if you don't pay attention. Move a router only in one direction—against the clockwise turn of the bit. The resistance steadies the rip guide against the post edge. Always hold the rip guide tight against the post as you work. When you get to the end of a groove, shut off the motor and hold the router still until the blade stops spinning.

**6** **ATTACH A STOP BOARD, AND ROUT.** Nail or screw a board near the top of the post to stop the groove at the desired height. Allow for the base plate; this router's base plate is 3 inches in radius, so the board is positioned 3 inches above the top of the planned groove. For the pattern shown, the board was positioned 8 inches below the post top to stop the two outer grooves 11 inches below the top; then it was moved 5 inches below the post top to stop the center groove 8 inches below the post top.

**7** **ADJUST POSTHOLES.** Dig extra-wide postholes for the 6 by 6s. Set one post at the desired height, and check for plumb in both directions as you tamp soil around it. Set the others in postholes, and use a level set atop a straight board to check the tops for level. Measure to find how much deeper or shallower the holes need to be, and dig or add and tamp soil as needed. Set the posts, and tamp soil around them to make them firm.

**8** **ADD THE NAILER AND TOP PIECES.**
For each post, cut and nail a 2 by 3 nailer on each side where the lattice will go. Position the top of the nailer ³/₄ inch below where you want the top of the lattice section to be. Cut two 1 by 4s for a cap rail and top rail to span between each pair of posts (measure near the bottom of the posts rather than the tops; you can adjust the posts slightly when you install the rails). Attach one to the top of the nailer, and the other to the side.

**9** **ATTACH THE HORIZONTAL SLATS.** These lattice slats are "self-spaced," meaning that you can simply use a slat as a spacer. Attach the slats with 2-inch finish nails driven into the nailers.

**10** **ADD THE VERTICAL SLATS.** Use the same spacing method for the vertical slats. Drive a ³/₄-inch staple or two ³/₄-inch finish nails into each joint. As you come within six or seven pieces of the end of a section, measure the remaining distance; you may choose to adjust the spacing slightly so things come out looking even.

**11** **FINISH WITH THE CAPS.** A decorative post cap will slip over a standard 6 by 6 —but not a rough-cut 6 by 6 like those shown here. If the posts you have chosen are too wide, cut a 2 by 6 to a length of 5¹/₂ inches to form a square block for each post. Nail the block to the post top, and attach the cap to the block. Prime and paint or stain and seal once the wood is dry.

# arbor
# projects

# KIT ARBORS

IF YOU CAN FIND A MANUFACTURED ARBOR THAT SUITS YOUR NEEDS AND SPEAKS TO YOUR SOUL, buying a kit may be your best option, especially if your woodworking skills are not strong. A trip to a home center or nursery may yield a modest selection of kit arbors; typing "arbors" into a search engine will give you hundreds more from which to choose.

Many kit arbors are made of clear (knot-free) Western red cedar, which is beautiful and somewhat resistant to rot. However, any portion that is sunk in the ground or that stays wet for long periods needs to be well protected with sealer. You can also find arbors made of vinyl or powder-coated metal; these require little maintenance and last a long time.

ABOVE: **This expansive arbor comes with a gate and two fence sections, which can be purchased separately. Made of vinyl, it will retain its clean looks for years with only an occasional washing.**

## Assembly

Determine ahead of time how you will attach the arbor. Some units come with stakes and others do not. If the stakes provided are unattractive, consider cutting cedar stakes to match; drive them into the ground next to the arbor, drill pilot holes, and drive screws to attach. You may be able to attach at least some of an arbor's legs to a landscaping timber using angle brackets and screws.

Assembling a kit arbor takes a bit more time than putting together a factory-made trellis (see pages 32–33). You will probably need a ladder, a drill with a screwdriver bit, and perhaps a hammer. If there are no pilot holes, take the time to drill them before driving any screws that are within 3 inches of the end of a board; otherwise, the board may split.

**FAR LEFT: An ornate metal arbor can add a formal or fanciful touch to a yard. Buy a unit with powder coating that is guaranteed against rust; cheaper units that are painted may flake and rust within a few years.**

**LEFT: A cedar arch is a no-brainer, welcome in almost any setting. This one is rich with corrosion-resistant natural oils; the wood will gradually weather over time to a silvery gray.**

# PATH HUGGER

THIS TRIM ARBOR WITH A CLASSIC DESIGN IS SIZED PERFECTLY FOR A NARROW PATHWAY. At 2 feet wide and 7 feet high, it's just right for a single person passing through and doesn't overwhelm a modest garden space.

This snug design uses small-dimensioned materials like 2 by 4 posts and arches made of ³/₄-inch plywood, but it is surprisingly firm when all the pieces are assembled. If you'd like a somewhat wider arbor, it can easily be modified—up to a point. The plywood arches cannot span more than 4 feet, measured between the outside of the posts, making for about 41 inches of width inside the structure.

## Getting Ready

If you want to make the structure stronger, consider setting the posts in concrete (see page 106). Use pressure-treated lumber for all the pieces except the cove molding, which is not available treated. The posts should be made of treated wood rated for ground contact. Plan to coat the cove molding with several coats of primer and paint.

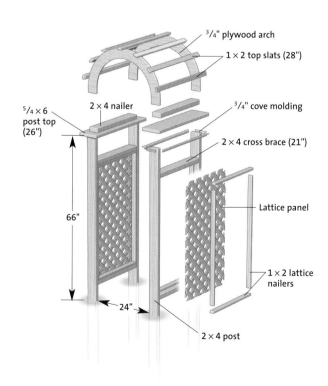

³/₄" plywood arch

1 × 2 top slats (28")

2 × 4 nailer

³/₄" cove molding

⁵/₄ × 6 post top (26")

2 × 4 cross brace (21")

Lattice panel

66"

1 × 2 lattice nailers

24"

2 × 4 post

## Materials List

- Four 8' 2 × 4 posts
- Two 8' 2 × 4s for cross braces and nailers
- One 6' ⁵/₄ × 6 for post tops
- Ten 8' 1 × 2s for lattice nailers and top slats
- One 12' piece of ³/₄" cove molding
- Half sheet of ³/₄" plywood for arches
- One sheet of vinyl lattice
- 3" decking or stainless-steel screws, 2" galvanized finish nails
- Exterior spackle or wood filler, primer, and paint

**1** **LAY OUT FOR THE ARCHES.** Snap a chalk line down the center of the plywood, and mark a line 24 inches (the distance between the insides of the posts) on the chalk line from the plywood edge. Tack a nail at the edge of the plywood on the chalk line. Attach a string (a chalk line works well) to the nail. Wrap the string around a pencil or a marking pen so it marks at the 24-inch mark, and use the string compass to draw a half circle. Use the same technique to draw a line that is $3\frac{1}{2}$ inches (the width of a 2 by 4) outside the first line.

### PRO TIP

Some 2 by 4s are actually slightly wider than $3\frac{1}{2}$ inches. Measure yours and cut your arches to match.

**2** **CUT THE ARCHES.** Use a high-quality jigsaw to cut the first arch. Hold the saw blade just to the inside of the first line and just to the outside of the second line, so the arch ends up a true $3\frac{1}{2}$ inches wide. Make a second arch using the first as a template.

**3** **SAND, FILL, AND SAND AGAIN.** Use a palm sander or a hand sander with 80-grit sandpaper to round the edges and smooth the faces of the arches. Treated plywood is often rough; fill in any splinters and indentations with exterior spackle or wood filler, and sand smooth after spackle dries.

**4** **LAY OUT AND DIG HOLES.** Use the factory edges of a sheet of plywood to help mark for holes that form a 2-foot square (see pages 154–155). In this example, 12-inch pavers make the layout easy to figure. Save pieces of sod, so you can fill in around the posts later. Dig holes 2 to 3 feet deep.

**5** **SET POSTS WITH CROSS BRACES.** Place the posts in the holes, and check that they are at least 66 inches tall relative to the highest point on the ground (you will cut them to height later). Cut four cross braces to 21 inches. Drive nails or drill pilot holes and drive screws to attach two cross braces to each pair of posts, 5 inches and 60 inches above the ground. Check that each cross brace is level, and that it is level with the corresponding cross brace on the other pair of posts. Check the posts for plumb in both directions as you fill the postholes and tamp the soil firm.

**6** **CUT THE POST TOPS.** Make a mark on one post 66 inches from the highest point on the ground. Use a carpenter's level to draw cut lines on all four posts. Cut the posts to height using a circular saw.

**7** **ADD THE POST TOPS.** For each set of posts, cut a ⁵⁄₄ by 6 decking board so it will overhang the sides of the posts by the same distance that it overhangs their front and back edges (typically, 1 inch). Attach it to the posts with screws. Cut a 2 by 4 nailer that is 1½ inches shorter than the distance between the outside edges of each pair of posts. Center the nailer on the decking board and attach it.

**8** **ATTACH THE ARCHES.** Drive 2-inch finish nails to attach an arch to one of the 2 by 4 nailers. Pull or push the post on the other side so the other nailer lines up with the other side of the arch, and drive nails to attach it. Install the other arch the same way.

**9** **ATTACH THE TOP SLATS.** Cut seven 1 by 2 slats so they overhang the arches by 2 inches on each side. Position a slat at the top center, overhanging equally past each arch, and drive finish nails to attach it. Using a ⁵⁄₄ by 6 scrap as a spacer, attach the other slats in the same way.

**10** **SANDWICH THE LATTICE.** Nail 1 by 2s to the posts and to the cross braces to one side of where the lattice will go. Cut a piece of vinyl lattice to fit. Place the lattice in the opening, and add a second set of 1 by 2s to sandwich the lattice (see pages 88–89). Install the lattice and 1 by 2s for the other set of posts.

**11** **TRIM WITH COVE.** Using a miter saw, cut pieces of cove molding to wrap around the underside of the ⁵⁄₄ by 6 board on each set of posts. Attach with finish nails or brads.

## BUILDING OPTIONS

If you plan to spray-paint the arbor, do so before installing the vinyl lattice. Or, you may choose to install one side of the lattice temporarily with a few tacked (partially driven) nails. Once the wood has dried, you can easily remove the lattice to paint the arbor.

# A SPACIOUS ARCHWAY

A ROOMY ARCH LIKE THIS CAN EASILY HOUSE A COUPLE OF LOUNGE CHAIRS, or simply allow plenty of space around a pathway. Its clean, stately lines make it at home in either a casual or a formal setting.

## Getting Ready

Cutting the 12 curved pieces, then assembling and smoothing the arches, takes four or more hours of painstaking work, though no special skills are needed. Allow yourself plenty of time, so you can take breaks to restore your concentration. The rest of the project is not especially difficult. You will need two sturdy ladders and a reliable helper when it comes time to attach the arches and the top slats.

Use pressure-treated lumber for the project; the posts should be rated for ground contact. Build the arches first, then dig holes and set posts to match the span of the arches.

## Materials List

- Four 8' 4 × 4 posts
- Six 10' 2 × 12s for the arches
- Two 10' 2 × 4s for the cross braces
- Two 10' 2 × 2s and ten 8' 2 × 2s for lattice framing and top slats
- One 10' 1 × 6 for trim
- Seven 10' 1 × 2s and five 8' 1 × 2s for lattice slats (perhaps ripped from 2 × 10s and 2 × 8s)
- One 4' 1 × 2 for trammel
- Plywood sheet for template
- 2½" and 3" decking or stainless-steel screws, 1¼" staples, 2" galvanized nails
- Exterior wood glue or polyurethane glue
- Exterior wood filler or spackle, primer, and paint

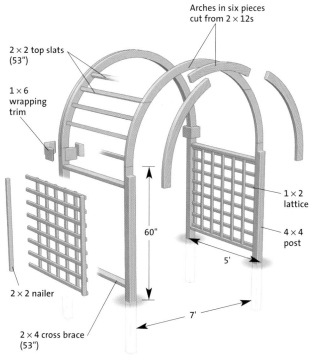

Arches in six pieces cut from 2 × 12s

2 × 2 top slats (53")

1 × 6 wrapping trim

1 × 2 lattice

4 × 4 post

60"

5'

2 × 2 nailer

2 × 4 cross brace (53")

7'

**1** **MAKE A PLYWOOD TEMPLATE.** First, make a trammel by cutting a 1 by 2 to about 4 feet and drilling holes at 1 inch, 43 inches, and 46½ inches. This will mark for a 3½-inch-wide arch that is 7 feet across on the inside (7 feet is two times 42 inches, the distance between the first two holes). Tack a nail through the 1-inch hole of the trammel near the center middle of the plywood sheet. Insert a pencil into the 43-inch hole and swing the trammel to mark that curve. Repeat with the third hole. Cut the template using a jigsaw.

**2** **ROUGH-CUT THE ARCH PIECES.** Cut pieces of 2 by 12 for each arch assembly. For the front face of each arch, cut two pieces to 48 inches with 22½-degree angles at one end, and one piece at 72 inches with straight-cut ends. For each rear face, cut two pieces to 60 inches and one piece to 39 inches with 30-degree angles at both ends.

**3** **MARK FOR THE CURVE CUTS.** Snug the pieces for each arch face against each other end to end. Place the plywood template on top, and use a pencil to mark for the curved cuts.

**4** **CUT THE CURVES.** You could attempt to cut the curves using a professional-quality jigsaw, but do so only if you are certain the saw will cut perfectly perpendicular to the face of the board. Any deviation from 90 degrees will be very noticeable when you laminate two boards together. Here we use a good-quality circular saw, which ensures a perpendicular cut. Cutting a sweeping curve like this is not as difficult as you might expect. Make the first pass with the blade set about ½ inch deep, a second with the blade at 1 inch, and a final cut with the blade at 1½ inches. Use a high-quality saw blade (a carbide blade with 24 or more teeth is a good choice), and don't be surprised if it becomes dull by the time you are done.

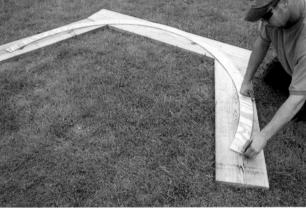

**5** **ASSEMBLE THE ARCHES.** Once all the pieces are cut, lay the rear-face pieces for one of the arches on a flat surface, and set the front-face pieces on top. (Don't cut the ends yet.) The pieces will probably not match perfectly at this point. Make sure, however, that the inside edges match closely; the outside edges will be easier to sand. Once you have the arrangement that fits best, remove one front-face piece, apply a squiggle of glue, set it back, drill pilot holes, and drive screws every 6 inches or so in an alternating pattern. Avoid placing screws too close to the ends of the arch pieces, which will be cut later.

**6** **SAND, FILL, AND SAND.** Use a belt sander with 60-grit paper to sand the sides. Sand in long, sweeping strokes; if you let the sander rest in one place for a second or two, it may dig in. You do not need to achieve perfection. Still, you may choose to apply exterior spackle or wood filler, then sand again. Cut the ends of the arch square, with the front face 4 inches longer at the bottom than the rear face. (To make the rear face cut, set your circular saw to the depth of that piece.)

**7** **SET THE POSTS.** Dig holes and set the posts (see pages 154–156), making sure the arches will span from post to post. Attach 2 by 4 cross braces about 3 inches and 53 inches above the ground. Set a level atop a long board to ensure that the cross braces are level with each other. Measure up from the cross braces to mark the post for cutting to height. Cut the posts 60 inches from the ground, then cut notches in the tops 4 inches long and $1^3/4$ inch deep, so the front face of the arch will rest in the notch.

**8** **ATTACH THE ARCHES.**
Working with a helper, place each arch on top of two posts. Drill three pilot holes and drive 3-inch screws to attach the arch at each end. Once both arches are in place, temporarily tack two 2 by 2s or other boards on top of the arches to keep them from wobbling as you work on the lattice. Make sure the front face of each arch is flush with the sides of the posts. Cover the joints between the arches and posts with 1 by 6 trim.

**9** **ADD THE LATTICE.** Cut and nail 2 by 2 nailers to fit between the 2 by 4 cross braces on each post. Lay out for evenly spaced horizontal 1 by 2s, and attach them to the nailers by power-nailing 2-inch galvanized finish nails or by drilling pilot holes and driving 2-inch screws. Lay out and cut evenly spaced vertical 1 by 2s and attach them to the horizontal 1 by 2s with 1¼-inch staples or screws.

**10** **ATTACH THE TOP SLATS.** Cut 2 by 2 slats to length, and drill angled pilot holes about 1½ inches from the board ends, using a countersink bit. Working with a helper, drive 3-inch screws to attach a slat at the center of the arches, positioning the screws on the tops. Use a 10-inch spacer to lay out for the remaining slats; you may need to adjust the spacing to achieve even spacing. You can add a decoration at the center of the arch as shown (see page 65). Once the wood dries, prime and paint it.

# GARDEN PORTAL

IF THIS DESIGN LOOKS FAMILIAR, THAT'S BECAUSE IT'S A CLASSIC THAT HAS BEEN AROUND FOR SOME TIME. The arches are made of three pieces each, with a clearly visible horizontal line between them. There is a pleasingly simple starburst design under each arch and trellises on each side so plants can climb up, and perhaps over, the arches.

## Getting Ready

Making a template for the arch pieces is a bit tricky, so Step 1 walks you through the process. Cutting the arches is easy as long as you have a good-quality jigsaw equipped with a heavy-duty blade. The rest of the project is straightforward.

It's common to paint this arbor, but you can apply stain and sealer instead. Either way, wait for the treated wood to dry before applying finish. Use treated 4 by 4 posts rated for ground contact and treated lumber for all the other pieces.

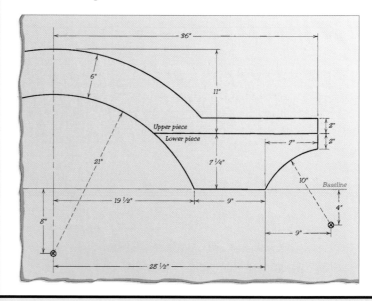

## Materials List

- Four 10' 4 × 4 posts
- Two 8' 2 × 12s for all the arch pieces
- One 8' 2 × 2 for two top slats
- One 8' 1 × 4 for top horizontals
- Twenty-four 8' 1 × 2s for lattice and starburst design

- Four decorative screw-in post caps
- 4 × 8 sheet of cardboard or plywood for template and trammels
- Eight ³/₈" x 5¹/₂" carriage bolts with washers and nuts
- 3" decking or stainless-steel screws, 2¹/₂" and 1¹/₄" galvanized finish nails or staples
- Exterior primer and paint

**1** **MAKE THE TEMPLATE.** A cardboard template works well and is easy to cut, but you can also use a plywood sheet (see page 81). Lay the cardboard on a flat wood surface, cut off any unneeded flaps, and draw a straight baseline at least 6 feet long about 10 inches from the bottom of the sheet. To make a trammel **(A)**, cut a cardboard strip 2 to 3 inches wide and 24 inches long. Mark it an inch or so from the bottom, then mark it 21 and 27 inches from the first point. Poke a pencil through the two upper marks, and poke a screw through the bottom one. Twist the screw through the trammel and into a point 8 inches below the baseline and in the center of the length of the cardboard.

Maintaining a grip on the screw head to keep the trammel from wandering, draw curves indicating the bottom and the top of the arch **(B)**. The lower curve meets with the baseline at each end, while the upper curve stops about 9 inches up from the baseline (you can erase or cross out overlapping lines later).

From the inside of the arch at the baseline, measure 9 inches over and make a mark indicating the start of the small curve. From that spot, measure another 9 inches across and 4 inches down to mark the center point of the small curve **(C)**.

Make a 10-inch trammel and draw the curve **(D)**. Mark for the other side the same way. Use the framing square to draw the vertical straight lines at the ends of the pieces; the upper piece and the lower pieces are all 2 inches wide at the outer edge.

Erase or cross out any lines that extend too far and double-check that the pattern matches the drawing at left. Use the cardboard trammel to cut the curves **(E)**: Holding the screw in place to keep the trammel from wandering, pierce with a utility knife through the trammel and the curved line at once, then cut the curve. Use the framing square as a guide to cut the straight lines. You will end up with three template pieces.

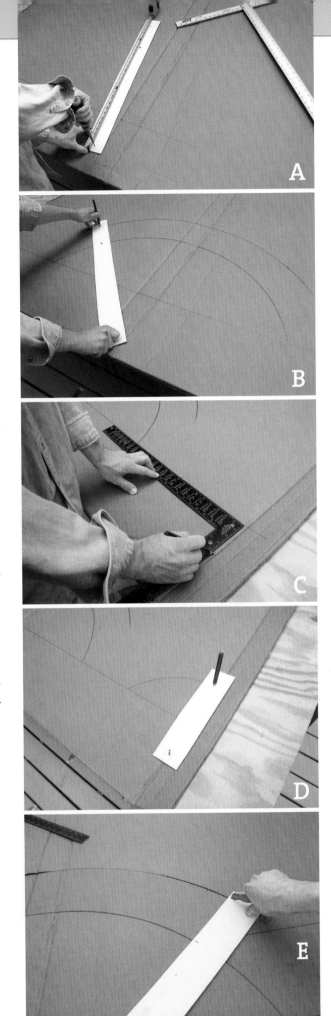

**2** **MARK FOR THE ARCH PIECES.** Place the cardboard templates on a 2 by 12. If possible, arrange them so you will not cut through a knot. Hold each piece firm so it does not move as you trace around it on the board.

**3** **CUT THE PIECES.** Check your circular saw and your jigsaw to make sure the blades are square to the base plates (see page 145). Cut the straight lines with the circular saw, then cut the curves with a jigsaw. Use the templates to mark for the second set of arch pieces and cut them as well.

**PRO TIP**

As you near the end of a cut with the jigsaw, make sure the waste side of the board is supported so it does not fall off, which could crack the board.

**4** **ASSEMBLE THE ARCHES.** Use a hand sander or palm sander to slightly round the cut edges of the arch pieces. Position a lower piece against an upper piece with the ends flush, drill pilot holes, and drive two 3-inch screws to attach the pieces together. Do the same for each lower piece.

**5** **SET AND CUT THE POSTS.** Lay an assembled arch on the ground and mark for the postholes. (Position the posts in relation to the arches as shown on page 84.) Lay out for the other two holes and dig all four holes (see pages 154–155). Set the posts in the holes, and fill with tamped soil, checking each post for plumb as you work. Use a carpenter's level or a small level atop a straight board to mark all four posts at the same height, and use a circular saw to cut them to height.

**6** **MAKE THE LATTICES.** For each set of posts, cut and attach 1 by 2 verticals flush with the outside edges and the tops of the posts. Check the posts for plumb, then cut a 1 by 4 horizontal that fits between the vertical 1 by 2s at the bottom. Attach it between the 1 by 2 verticals at the top. Experiment to find a consistent spacing for three 1 by 2 verticals in between, and cut a spacer to this measurement. Use the spacer to install the verticals. Cut and install the horizontals, beginning at the top.

**7** **ATTACH THE ARCHES.** Check the posts for plumb again. Working with a helper, position the arch so it is flush with the posts at the top, and the bottom of the small curve is flush with the outside of the post (you may need to adjust the position slightly). Drive a 3-inch screw into each post or use clamps to hold the arch in place while you work. Drill holes for the carriage bolts; you may need to remove the arch to finish drilling the holes. Pound the bolts through the holes, add washers, and tighten the nuts. For added stability, drive three more screws. Repeat for the other arch.

**8** **ADD THE STARBURSTS.** Cut and attach a horizontal 1 by 2 against the back side of each arch. Rip-cut a 1 by 2 in half to make the narrow starburst pieces. Install one piece in the center of each arch, checking it for plumb. Hold another at a pleasing angle and mark it for angled cuts at each end; use this as a template for the remaining three pieces, and attach them with nails.

**9** **TOP OFF.** Cut two 2 by 2s to fit between the arches; drill steeply angled pilot holes and drive screws to attach the slats. Drill holes down through the tops of the posts and screw in the decorative post caps. Once the wood has dried, apply primer and paint.

# AN ELEGANT ARBOR NOOK

WHAT BETTER PLACE TO SIT AND WATCH THE STARS COME OUT THAN ON THIS ARBOR-TOPPED COURTING BENCH? It's freestanding, so you can even move it around from time to time—with the help of a few friends, since it is a substantial structure. Better yet, keep it in one spot and plant vines to climb up the lattice and over the top, providing a shady retreat on hot summer afternoons.

## Getting Ready

Build the components on a flat floor, then assemble them on-site. To get the appealing dark look shown here, use pressure-treated lumber and stain after the wood has dried, using a stain made specifically to make green treated wood look like cedar or redwood (see page 158). Or, use the dark heartwood of cedar or redwood. Because people will sit on and handle all the parts except the beams and slats overhead, choose lumber that is free of splinters and cracks, and sand the edges thoroughly.

This bench seat is 60 inches long and 18 inches deep, an area that will accommodate many seat cushions you can buy at a home center or patio furniture store. If the cushions of your choice are a different size, adjust the size of the seat frame (see Step 4).

## Materials List

- Four 8' 4 × 4 posts
- Five 10' 2 × 4s for framing members and seat pieces
- Nine 8' 2 × 6s for beams and seat pieces (rip the 1 × 2s out of two of the 2 × 6s)
- Two heavy-duty (³/₄") lattice panels
- 3" and 2¹/₂" decking or stainless-steel screws, 3¹/₂" galvanized framing nails, 1¹/₄" and 2" galvanized finish nails or staples
- Eight ³/₈" × 5¹/₂" carriage bolts with washers and nuts
- Sixteen ³/₄" copper pipe endcaps (about 1" outside diameter)
- Polyurethane glue
- Exterior stain and sealer

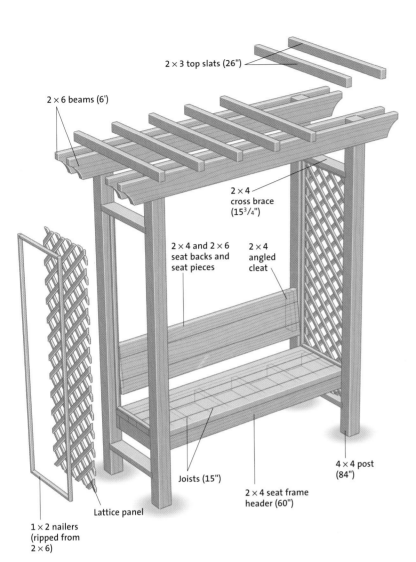

2 × 3 top slats (26")

2 × 6 beams (6')

2 × 4 cross brace (15³⁄₄")

2 × 4 and 2 × 6 seat backs and seat pieces

2 × 4 angled cleat

4 × 4 post (84")

Joists (15")

2 × 4 seat frame header (60")

Lattice panel

1 × 2 nailers (ripped from 2 × 6)

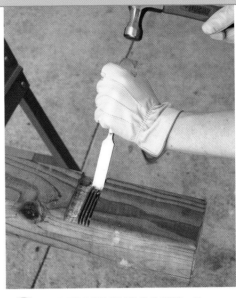

**1** **PREPARE THE POSTS.** Cut the four posts to 84 inches. Place them precisely side by side, and mark for two 1¹⁄₂-inch-wide notches, with their bottoms at 6 and 70 inches from the post bottoms. Use a board to check that the notches will be wide enough to accommodate 2 by 4 cross braces. Set a circular saw blade to cut ³⁄₈ inch deep and cut the lines on either side of each notch. Cut a series of lines in the middle, and clean out the notches with a chisel. Or, use a router, as shown on page 153.

**2** **BUILD THE SIDE FRAMES.** Cut four 2 by 4 cross braces to 15³⁄₄ inches. On a flat surface, assemble each side frame by slipping the cross braces into the notches on two posts. Check for square, then drill pilot holes and drive 3-inch screws.

**3** **ADD THE LATTICE.** Cut 1 by 2 nailers to fit inside each side frame, just outside where the lattice will go. Attach them with 2-inch nails. For each frame, cut a sheet of lattice to fit, set it on top of the 1 by 2s, and attach it with 1¹⁄₄-inch finish nails or staples.

**4** **BUILD THE SEAT FRAME.** To make a seat frame measuring 18 inches by 60 inches, cut two headers to 60 inches and six joists to 15 inches. Mark the headers for joists placed at each end and evenly spaced in between. Attach with screws or framing nails.

**5** **ATTACH THE SEAT TO THE SIDE FRAMES.** Mark for the position of the seat frame and attach 1 by 2 pieces to complete the lattice sandwich, allowing room for the 1½-inch-thick seat pieces that will be installed later. Working with a helper, lay the side frames on their sides, and slip the seat frame into the side frames. Check the structure for square, then drill pilot holes and drive two 3-inch screws into each joint to attach the seat frame to the four posts.

**6** **CUT THE BEAMS.** Cut four 2 by 6 beams to 84 inches long. For the pattern shown, use a square to draw a 2-inch line parallel to the top of the beam and 1½ inches from the top. Draw a perpendicular 2-inch line 4 inches from the end. Use a paint can to connect the two lines. See page 149 for other ideas on cutting decorative ends.

### PRO TIP

The seat pieces will need gaps for water to run through. If the wood is wet, install the boards with no gaps, as shown here; the boards will shrink to produce ⅛-inch gaps. If the wood is already dry, use nails or other spacers to make ⅛-inch gaps between the boards when you install them.

**7** **ATTACH SEAT PIECES AND THE BACK CLEATS.** Cut seat pieces—two 2 by 6s and two 2 by 4s—to fit snugly against the lattice and attach them with 3-inch screws. Add 1 by 2s on the inside of the frame to finish sandwiching the lattice. Cut two angled 2 by 4 cleats, making each one 12 inches long, 3½ inches wide at the bottom, and 2 inches wide at the top. This will make for a seat back that angles back slightly. Position each cleat about four inches above the seat (higher if your cushion is very plush), its back flush with the back of the post. Attach by drilling three pilot holes and driving 3-inch screws.

**8**  **ADD THE BACK PIECES.**
Cut two 2 by 4s and one 2 by 6 to form the seat back. Attach them to the cleats by drilling pilot holes and driving 3-inch screws.

**9**  **PREPARE THE BEAMS.**
Mark each beam for bolts that will be centered on the posts, 2 inches from the top and bottom. Before drilling the holes, use a 1-inch spade bit on a scrap piece of wood to confirm that the copper caps will fit snugly in the holes you drill. Then mark the bit at the desired depth and drill countersink holes for the bolts. Clamp the beams in place at the top of the posts, one on each side of each set of posts, drill ³⁄₈-inch holes from either side, and tap in carriage bolts.

**10**  **TAP IN COPPER CAPS AND FINISH.**
For each bolt hole, squirt in a bit of polyurethane glue and tap in a copper cap. Cut and install the 2 by 3 top slats so they are evenly spaced and overhang both sides by 6 inches. Sand the edges of the assembly smooth and apply sealer and stain once the wood is dry.

# TUNNEL ARBOR

WITH ITS SOARING ARCHES AND PRECISE GEOMETRY, this long, tunnel-like arbor lends an air of formal elegance to your outdoor environment. Build it to lead to one of your garden's visual highlights, or simply top off one of your walkways to offer an enticing way to get from one place to another. As climbing plants grow over the framework, a walk through the tunnel will provide an intimate garden experience.

As you might guess from the photograph, a tunnel arbor is not quick and easy. But don't let that stop you. The project can be broken down into a number of steps that require only medium carpentry skills.

Two details make this arbor inviting: the square edges of the pieces, and the geometric precision with which they are assembled. The crisp, clean look comes from rip-cutting standard 2 by 4s so they have sharply squared edges. You will need a table saw (see pages 146–147). If you want the cut edges to be factory-smooth, use a jointer or a belt sander.

## Getting Ready

The steps described here are for a 58-inch-long, 4-foot-wide tunnel arbor consisting of four arched side panels (two per side) fastened together with a series of filler pieces.

## Materials List

- One 10' 4 × 4, rated for ground contact, for two bottom runners
- Eleven 8' 2 × 4s for uprights, long fillers, short fillers, and blocks
- Two sheets of ³/₄" pressure-treated plywood
- Five 6' 1 × 2s, perhaps rip-cut from 2 × 4s or 2 × 6s, for slats
- Four 2' pieces of ¹/₂" rebar
- 1¹/₄", 2¹/₂", and 3¹/₂" decking or stainless-steel screws
- Exterior wood glue or polyurethane glue
- Exterior wood filler, primer, and paint
- Gravel

## MATERIALS TIP

On a project like this, the quality of the lumber makes all the difference. Select your 2 by 4s carefully, looking for pieces that are very straight and free of cracks or large knots. You may want to use a high-grade lumber such as KDAT or Select (see page 139).

For a longer arbor, simply add side panels, fillers, and the top pieces and bottom runners to go with them. Each filler and side panel combination will add 35 inches to the length of your tunnel.

Use pressure-treated lumber and plywood. (Marine-grade plywood is smoother than standard treated plywood, but it is expensive and may be hard to find.) The bottom runners should be made of lumber rated for ground contact. Prime and paint as many pieces as possible before assembly, then give the whole structure a finish coat.

These pages show attaching with screws, but you may want to use a power framing nailer instead (see page 150). Hand-nailing would cause the structure to wobble as you work and is not recommended.

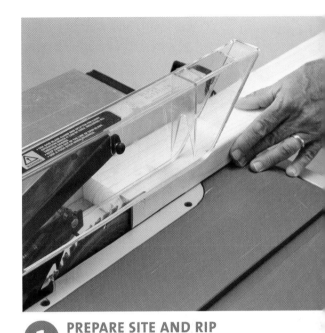

**1 PREPARE SITE AND RIP BOARDS.** Dig a 6-inch-wide, 6-inch-deep trench on each side of your arbor pathway, spacing the trenches 45 inches apart on center and extending them the length of the planned arbor. Fill the trenches with gravel and tamp it firm using a hand tamper or a 2 by 4. Cut the arbor's bottom runners and place them in the gravel with their outer edges 48 inches apart. Check that the runners rest on gravel all along their lengths. Each runner does not need to be level, but the two runners should be level with each other at every point. Drill ½-inch holes through each runner about 6 inches from each end and drive pieces of rebar to anchor the runners.

Next, prepare the 2 by 4s. With a table saw, rip-cut ¼ inch off each side to eliminate the rounded corners and make the pieces just 3 inches wide. If you have access to a jointer, use it to remove the saw marks. Or use a belt sander, holding the belt flat on the wood at all times to avoid gouging the wood.

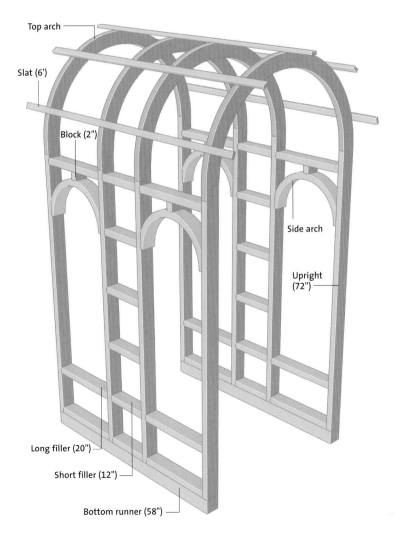

Top arch

Slat (6')

Block (2")

Side arch

Upright (72")

Long filler (20")

Short filler (12")

Bottom runner (58")

**2** **CUT THE PIECES.** Cut the narrowed 2 by 4s to length. You'll need eight 72-inch uprights, twelve 20-inch fillers, twelve 12-inch fillers, and four 2-inch blocks. Take care to make the cuts precisely square; a power miter saw makes this easy, but you can do it with a circular saw and an angle square, as shown.

**3** **NOTCH THE UPRIGHTS.** Cut a $1\frac{1}{2}$-inch-wide by 3-inch-long notch in the top of each upright. These notches will serve as the attachment points for the arches that span the pathway. Measure and cut precisely, using a circular saw or a power miter saw first and then a jigsaw.

**4** **BUILD THE SIDE PANELS.** Assemble the side panels by drilling pilot holes and driving $3\frac{1}{2}$-inch screws to attach the long fillers in place between pairs of uprights. Position the bottom fillers flush with the bottoms of the uprights, the middle fillers 12 inches above the bottom ones, and the top fillers $4\frac{1}{2}$ inches below the tops of the uprights. For consistency, cut a piece of scrap lumber 12 inches long as a spacer to locate the middle fillers above the bottom ones.

**5** **CUT THE SIDE ARCHES.** The side arches are made from four layers of $\frac{3}{4}$-inch plywood. Cut a sheet of plywood 55 inches long. (Save the remaining portion for the top arches.) Draw lines down the plywood lengthwise to establish two 20-inch-wide strips, plus a strip of scrap. Draw a center line down the middle of each strip. Measure $10\frac{3}{4}$ inches from one end to mark the center of the first arch layer. To lay out the inner and outer curves, make a trammel from a piece of wood or a yardstick and two trammel points, setting the points $10\frac{3}{4}$ inches apart for the outside arc and $9\frac{1}{4}$ inches apart for the inside arc. For the center of each subsequent arch layer, measure $6\frac{1}{2}$ inches down the center line from the previous center point. You should get eight arch layers from each strip. Note that the arch layers will have a flat area on either side. Cut the arch layers using a jigsaw.

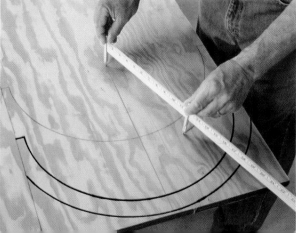

**6** **ASSEMBLE THE SIDE PANELS.** Glue and screw the side arch pieces together with 1¼-inch screws about 3 inches apart, countersinking the screws. Screw the second arch layer to the first layer, the third to the second, and so on. Sand and fill the arches as needed. Screw the blocks to the arches, then position the arches inside the side panels and screw them in place using 2½-inch screws. Drill pilot holes to avoid splitting the plywood.

**7** **COMPLETE THE SIDES.** Join each set of two panels by screwing the short fillers in between them, drilling pilot holes and driving 3½-inch screws. Position the bottom filler flush with the bottoms of the uprights, and then space all the fillers but the top one 12 inches apart; the top filler should align with the top filler pieces in the side panels. For four of the fillers, you'll need to drill angled pilot holes through the uprights into the filler ends. Drive two screws per joint.

**8** **ADD THE TOP ARCHES.** The top arches are made from two layers of plywood. The outer radius is 24 inches, the inner one 21 inches. After you cut the first arch layer, use it as a template to trace for the subsequent layers. Glue and screw together each pair of arch layers with 1¼-inch screws.

Cut 1½-inch-wide by 3-inch-long notches in each end to match the notches in the uprights. Then prime and paint the arches and sides. Position the arbor sides on the bottom runners, outside edges flush. Drive 2½-inch screws through the bottom fillers into the runners. Drill pilot holes and screw the top arches to the uprights with 2½-inch screws. Screw the slats to the top arches, about 12¼ inches apart on center. Fill the screw holes before giving the entire assembly a final coat of paint.

# ARBOR WITH BENCH

A GARDEN BENCH SITUATED UNDER A VINE-BEDECKED ARBOR—what's not to like? Find a secluded corner of your garden and install this classic combination to create a quiet retreat from the rigors of everyday life.

## Getting Ready

Building a bench and arbor combo is in some ways less complicated than building a standalone bench. The arbor provides the structure, and the bench comes along for the ride with no complex angles or fancy joinery. Where we show joining pieces with a pair of carriage bolts, you may choose instead to drive four 3-inch decking screws or two lag screws.

Use rot-resistant wood for all the members. The posts and the bench legs should be made of pressure-treated lumber that is rated for ground contact. If you use cedar, redwood, or above-ground-rated lumber, apply extra sealer.

If you want to pave the arbor floor, do so right after setting the posts. This will give you a hard surface from which to measure.

## Materials List

- Four 10' 4 × 4 posts
- Two 8' 2 × 6 beams
- One 12' 2 × 6 for three cross braces
- One 8' 2 × 6 for two seat supports and three back supports
- Two 8' 2 × 4s for four bench legs, back rail, and lattice support
- One 12' 2 × 8 for three seat planks
- One 8' 1 × 4 for two backrests

- One 4' 1 × 6 for two armrests
- Twelve 6' 2 × 2s for four verticals and eight slats
- One 4' × 4' lattice sheet, cut to 3' × 4'
- Four decorative corner braces
- ¼" galvanized carriage bolts with nuts and washers: four at 3½", eight at 5", four at 6"
- Twelve ¼" × 4" galvanized lag screws with washers
- 1¼" and 3" decking or stainless-steel screws
- Exterior stain and sealer or primer and paint

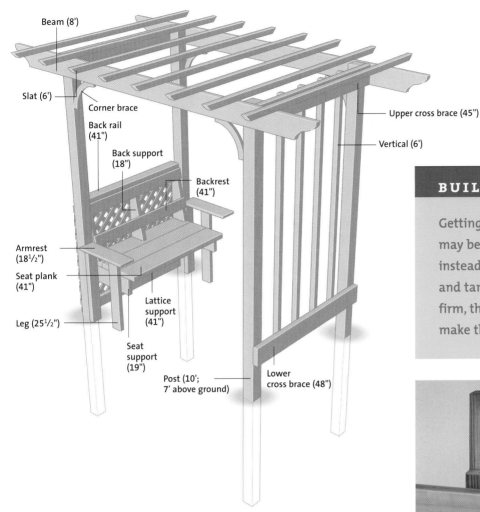

Beam (8')

Slat (6')

Corner brace

Back rail (41")

Back support (18")

Backrest (41")

Armrest (18½")

Seat plank (41")

Leg (25½")

Lattice support (41")

Seat support (19")

Post (10'; 7' above ground)

Lower cross brace (48")

Upper cross brace (45")

Vertical (6')

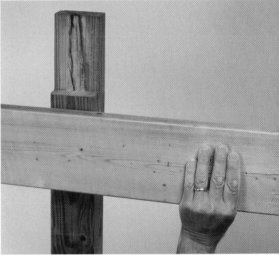

## BUILDING OPTION

Getting posts to the same height may be difficult. You may choose instead to set unnotched posts and tamp the soil to hold them firm, then cut them to height and make the notches.

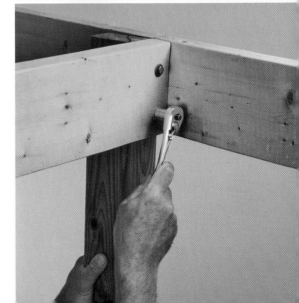

**1 NOTCH FOR BEAMS.** Cut 5½-inch-long by 1½-inch-deep notches in the tops of the posts, as shown on page 110. Lay out the site and dig holes for posts that form a rectangle 5 feet by 4 feet (see pages 154–156). Adjust the heights of the posts so the shoulders of the notches are level with each other. Tamp the soil or temporarily brace the posts in position.

Cut the ends of the 2 by 6 beams to a decorative profile (see page 149). Seat the beams in the post notches and center them from side to side. Bolt the beams to the posts with two 5-inch carriage bolts at each joint.

**2 ADD CROSS BRACES.** Cut the cross braces to length as shown in the diagram above and attach them to the posts by drilling holes and driving lag screws. Two cross braces attach to the tops of the posts; the third (longer) one goes on the end of the arbor opposite the bench, positioned 12 inches above the ground.

**3** **INSTALL SEAT SUPPORTS.** Cut the seat supports and back supports to length. Position each seat support beside a post with the top of the support 16½ inches above the ground and one end flush with the outside of the post. Drill a single ¼-inch hole through the post and the support, then bolt them together with a 6-inch carriage bolt. Adjust the support so it is level. Drill a ¼-inch hole and add a second carriage bolt.

**4** **INSTALL THE LEGS.** Bolt the front legs to the outside of the seat supports with 3½-inch carriage bolts, placing the legs 2 inches back from the front edges of the seat supports. Check that the legs are at least fairly plumb. Attach the back legs to the post with 3-inch screws.

**5** **ADD THE SEAT.** Cut the 2 by 8 into three 41-inch planks for the seat. Set the planks in place on the seat supports so that the back edge of the seat is flush with the outside of the posts. Leave a slight gap between the planks for drainage. Attach the planks with 3-inch screws. Round the corners with a jigsaw, then use a router with a ½-inch roundover bit to round off the edges.

**6** **ATTACH BACK SUPPORTS.** Cut the 18-inch-long back supports so they taper from 5½ inches at the bottom to 2 inches at the top. Align the back edge of the supports with the back of the seat and attach the supports to the post by drilling pilot holes and driving 3-inch screws. Attach the center back support by driving screws up through the seat from underneath.

**7** **ADD THE BACKRESTS.** Cut the back rail and backrests to length. Attach the back rail to the top of the back supports with 3-inch screws. (It will stick out behind the outside of the posts.) Screw the top backrest flush with the top ends of the back supports. Attach the second backrest between the top backrest and the seat.

**8** **INSTALL THE ARMRESTS.** Cut the armrests to length and round their front corners with a jigsaw. Use a router equipped with a ⅜-inch roundover bit to round the edges, then sand any rough edges. Attach the armrests to the tops of the legs with 3-inch screws, aligning the inside edges of the armrests with the inside faces of the front legs.

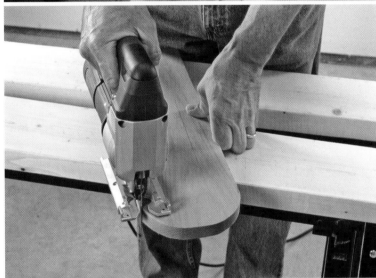

**9** **ADD LATTICE AND FINAL PIECES.** Cut the lattice supports to fit snugly between the posts behind the bench. Attach by drilling angled pilot holes and driving 3-inch screws. Cut the lattice panel to fit, and attach by driving 1¼-inch screws into the posts and supports.

Use a power miter saw or a circular saw to cut the ends of the 2 by 2 verticals and slats at a decorative angle. Using 3-inch screws, fasten the four verticals in place inside the cross braces on the side opposite the bench. Screw the eight slats on top of the beams. Screw the decorative corner braces in place. Finish the arbor with stain, or apply primer and paint.

# ROCKIN' ARBOR

HERE'S A RECIPE THAT CAN'T BE BEAT: Take one arbor; mix in a porch swing, a hot summer afternoon, and your favorite book. Season to taste with a tall glass of your favorite beverage and start rocking. Life just doesn't get more relaxing.

Unfortunately, a swing can't be hung in the air; it needs sturdy support, especially if rambunctious children will play on it. An arbor that supports a swing must be made of serious lumber and must be well anchored to the ground. This plan uses hefty 6 by 6s for the posts, beams, and swing-holders, as well as a commercially made porch swing.

## Getting Ready

Use pressure-treated lumber for all the parts. It may take time and patience to find 6 by 6s that are straight, relatively crack-free, and low in moisture content (see page 141). Sorting through the timbers may be a pain, but it is well worth the trouble. The posts should be rated for ground contact; if they are not, apply extra sealer (see page 45) to the ends that go into the ground. Because the posts are so heavy, sinking them only 2 feet in the ground will provide adequate insurance against wobbling while the swing is in action.

Building this project calls for only basic carpentry skills, but you will be working with heavy boards. Connections are made with heavy-duty lag screws and carriage bolts. Have helpers on hand, as well as a stable stepladder or two.

## Materials List

- Four 8' 2 × 4s for twelve cross braces
- Four 10' 6 × 6 posts
- Three 8' 6 × 6s for two beams and two swing-holders
- $^3/_8$" galvanized carriage bolts with nuts and washers: eight at 6", eight at 9"
- $3^1/_2$" galvanized finish nails
- Eight $^3/_8$" × 6" galvanized lag screws with washers
- Two $^3/_8$" × 8" galvanized eyebolts with nuts and lock washers
- Exterior primer and paint
- Porch swing

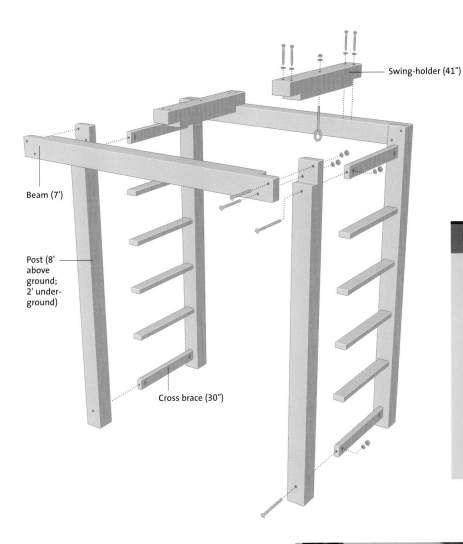

Swing-holder (41")

Beam (7')

Post (8' above ground; 2' under-ground)

Cross brace (30")

## BUILDING OPTIONS

You may choose to lay out and dig the 2-foot-deep holes, then install and temporarily brace each ladder section in the holes. Then you can attach the beams and swing-holders. Or, as shown on these pages, build the entire structure and move it onto the site to mark for the postholes.

**1 PREPARE FOUR CROSS BRACES.** Cut four of the cross braces shown in the diagram above. Drill 1-inch holes 4 inches from the ends of each piece, centered side to side. As soon as the bit pokes through the opposite side, turn the piece over and finish the hole from that side. This will help keep the wood from tearing out at the back of the hole. Use a file or rasp to form each hole into a D shape by flattening the side closest to the end of the cross brace. Next, drill ⅜-inch holes in the ends of the pieces, centering the holes and extending them all the way into the D-shaped holes.

**2** **ATTACH THE CROSS BRACES.**
Drill two $^3/_8$-inch holes through each post, placed $7^1/_4$ inches and $91^1/_4$ inches from the post top. Both holes should be centered from side to side. Counterbore each hole with a 1-inch bit to a depth of 1 inch to allow room to countersink the bolt heads. Slide 9-inch carriage bolts through the holes and into the holes you have drilled in the cross braces. Working within the D-shaped holes in the cross braces, place a washer and nut on the end of each bolt and tighten the nut with a wrench.

**3** **ADD THE OTHER CROSS BRACES.** Cut the rest of the cross braces. Position them between the posts, spaced about 15 inches apart. While the bolted cross braces are installed face out, these should be turned and installed edge out. You may find it helpful to cut two 15-inch lengths of scrap lumber to serve as spacers to keep the cross braces correctly aligned as you install them. To firmly attach a cross brace to the posts, drill angled pilot holes and drive two toenails from above (see page 151). Also drill an angled pilot hole and drive a nail from the bottom side of the cross brace. If you are hand-nailing, use a nailset for the final blow in each case to keep from marring the wood.

**4** **NOTCH THE POSTS AND BEAMS.**
To create the corner joints, lay out the notches on the beam ends and the post tops. Each notch is $2^3/_4$ inches deep (half the post's thickness), and $5^1/_2$ inches long (the width of the adjoining piece). Set a circular saw to cut the notch shoulders $2^3/_4$ inches deep. If your saw won't cut that deep, set it to full depth, make the cut, and finish with a handsaw. Cut in from the ends with a circular saw, then finish the cut using a handsaw.

**5** **INSTALL THE BEAMS.** Working with helpers, prop the post-and-cross brace assemblies upright, either in the postholes or on a flat surface (see tip, page 101). Set the first beam in place. Drill a $^3/_8$-inch hole through each joint and bolt the pieces together with 6-inch carriage bolts, washers, and nuts. Set the second beam in place and repeat the process. Double-check to make sure each beam is square to the legs, then drill the second set of carriage-bolt holes and finish bolting the beams and posts together.

**6** **ADD THE SWING.** Cut the swing-holders to fit on top of the beams. Notch the ends the same way you made the notches in Step 4, but make these notches only $1^1/_2$ inches deep. Measure carefully to find the center point of each swing-holder. Drill a $^3/_8$-inch hole through each holder at its center point. Push an eyebolt through the hole and fix it in place with a lock washer and nut. Position the swing-holders on top of the arbor and screw them to the beams with two lag screws at each end. Prime and paint the arbor. Then hang the swing from the eyebolts, priming and painting if needed.

**SAFETY** TIP

Check the hardware and framing at the start of each season and tighten any loose bolts.

# HAMMOCK DREAMS

WHENEVER YOU CAN GET DOUBLE DUTY FROM A PIECE OF GARDEN ARCHITECTURE, YOU ARE AHEAD OF THE GAME. And when you couple shade with a hammock… well, that's about as good as it gets. The only drawback will be having to settle disputes over whose turn it is for a nap.

## Getting Ready

Stout 4 by 6 posts of pressure-treated wood form the backbone of this arbor. If you prefer cedar or redwood, which are not as strong, you should use 6 by 6s instead. Here we show making decorative cuts on the tops of the posts, which means you will need to dig the holes at uniform depths so the posts will be at the same height. You could instead choose to set undecorated posts in holes, then cut them to height and add post tops.

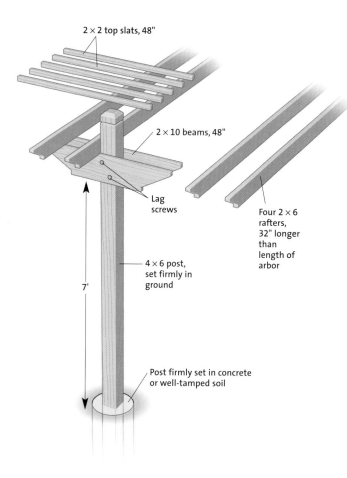

2 × 2 top slats, 48"

2 × 10 beams, 48"

Lag screws

Four 2 × 6 rafters, 32" longer than length of arbor

4 × 6 post, set firmly in ground

7'

Post firmly set in concrete or well-tamped soil

## Materials List

- Two 12' 4 × 6 posts
- Two 8' 2 × 10s for beams
- Four 14' 2 × 6s for rafters
- Twenty or more 8' 1 × 2s or 2 × 2s for top slats, depending on spacing
- Eight $^3/_8$" × 4" lag screws with washers
- 3" decking or stainless-steel screws
- Four or more 80-pound bags of "high early" (or "professional strength") concrete mix

**1** **ADORN THE POST TOPS.** To bevel-cut each post top, use an angle square to draw lines around the post ³/₄ inch from the top. Set a circular saw to a 45-degree angle and cut along the lines. To make the decorative groove, measure 4 inches down from the bottom of the bevel and use the square to draw two lines ¹/₄ inch apart around the post. Set the circular saw back to a 90-degree (straight) angle and cut to a depth of ¹/₂ inch. Cut both lines, then make a series of cuts to clean out the inside of the groove.

> **PRO TIP**
>
> Most hammocks require the posts to be at least 12 feet apart; the arbor here has posts 13 feet apart. Check your hammock's specs before building.

**2** **DIG LARGE HOLES.** Dig the postholes (see pages 154–156). Because the entire structure (and the person in the hammock) will be supported by only two posts, the concrete-filled postholes must be deep and wide. In normal soil, they should be at least 36 inches deep and 10 inches in diameter. If your soil is sandy, check with a local builder or building inspector for recommended hole sizes. For firm soil with a high clay component, you can fill the holes with firmly tamped soil instead of concrete if you dig the holes 48 inches deep (you will likely need a power auger).

**3** **CUT THE BEAMS.** Cut four 2 by 10 beams to 48 inches. To make the decorative end cut shown here, mark each end 1¹/₄ inches from the top. Mark the bottom 12 inches from the end and draw a 1¹/₄-inch line parallel to the end. Mark a straight line from the top mark to the top of the short line. Cut with a circular saw, taking care not to go past the intersections of lines. Finish the cuts using a jigsaw.

**4** **MARK FOR THE LAG SCREWS.** Clamp a beam to the post 12 inches below the decorative groove; measure to see that it is centered from side to side. Make two X marks for the lag screws, 1¹/₂ inches from the sides of the post, with one 1¹/₂ inches from the top and one 1¹/₂ inches from the bottom of the beams.

**5** **DRILL HOLES AND DRIVE LAG SCREWS.** Using a 1-inch spade bit, drill countersink holes ³⁄₈ inch deep. Drill pilot holes for the lag screws. Insert a washer into each countersink hole, and use a hammer and then a ratchet wrench to drive the lag screws.

**6** **CHECK ALIGNMENT AND ATTACH THE SECOND BEAM.** Turn the post upside down and install the second beam. Use a framing square to see that it is aligned with the other beam at the top and at the ends, then clamp it into place and repeat Step 5.

**7** **SET THE POSTS.** Place the posts in the holes and check that the tops are close to level with each other; you may need to dig one hole deeper. With a helper, lift each post a foot or so and drop it into the hole several times to tamp the soil at the bottom. Temporarily brace each post so it is plumb in both directions. Pour a bag of concrete mix into a wheelbarrow and slowly add water as you mix it with a shovel, scraping the bottom of the barrow as you work. Once the concrete is just pourable, tilt the wheelbarrow and scrape the concrete into the hole. You will probably need two bags per hole.

**8** **FINISH THE CONCRETE.** Mound the concrete slightly, using a trowel or a small board to smooth its surface. Bevel the concrete at a slight downward angle so rainwater will run away from the post. Allow the concrete to cure for at least a full day before working further on the arbor.

**9** **CUT THE RAFTERS.** Cut the 2 by 6 rafters so they will overhang the beams by 16 inches or so. To make the decorative cut shown here, make a mark 1 inch down from the top at the end of the board. Measure 7 inches along the bottom from the end and use a square to make a vertical line 1 inch long. Draw a straight line between the top mark and the top of the short line. Cut with a circular saw, then finish the cuts with a jigsaw.

**10** **ATTACH THE RAFTERS.** Mark the rafters for the desired overhang. Install the inner rafters by screwing them to the sides of the post. Install the outer rafters by drilling angled pilot holes and driving 3-inch screws into the beams.

**PRO TIP**

Most boards are not perfectly straight; they have a crown—a bend along their edge (see page 141). Sight along a rafter board to find the crown side, and always install the rafter with the crown side up.

**11** **ADD THE TOP SLATS.** Determine how far apart you want the top slats to be spaced. Make one spacer for this, and another to measure for the overhang beyond the outside rafter. Drill pilot holes and drive 3-inch screws to attach the slats to the rafters.

# GATEWAY ARBOR

AN ARCHED GATEWAY WITH A PICKET-FENCE GATE, painted a pristine white, captures a classic bit of Americana and speaks of a simpler time. This version features a pair of inviting arches resting atop stout 4 by 4 posts. A series of 1 by 4 slats connects the arches, forming a short tunnel and providing support for climbing plants. A single hinged gate completes the unit.

## Getting Ready

The most demanding part of the project is making the two arches, so build them first, then lay out and construct the rest of the project to fit the arches. You'll need to make a number of precise angled cuts as well as smooth curved cuts, so you'll need a power miter saw and a good-quality jigsaw.

Each arch is made from two layers of short 1 by 6 pieces, their ends cut at a 22.5-degree angle and butted together to form the curve. The pieces in the two layers are staggered, much like bricks are laid, to offset and reinforce the joints. There are four arch segments in each outside layer and five in each inside layer. At either end of the arch, the pieces in the inside layer extend to lap with straight sections. The result is a 1½-inch-thick arch. The arches in turn are attached to 4 by 4 posts that set in the ground.

## Materials List

- Two 10' 4 × 4s for four posts
- Two 8' 1 × 6s and two 10' 1 × 6s for eighteen arch segments
- Two 6' 1 × 4s for eight straight sections
- Nine 8' 1 × 4s for twenty-five slats
- One 8' 2 × 4 and one 10' 2 × 4 for the gate frame
- Three 10' 1 × 3s for eight gate pickets
- 1¼", 2", and 4" decking or stainless-steel screws
- Gate hinges and latch
- Exterior wood glue or polyurethane glue
- Exterior wood filler, primer, and paint

## BUILDING OPTIONS

These pages show building arches by cutting a number of pieces out of 1 by 6s, then laminating them in two overlapping layers. Arches can also be made of plywood (pages 92–95; use two layers to produce 1½-inch-thick arches) or from pieces of 2 by 12s (pages 80–83).

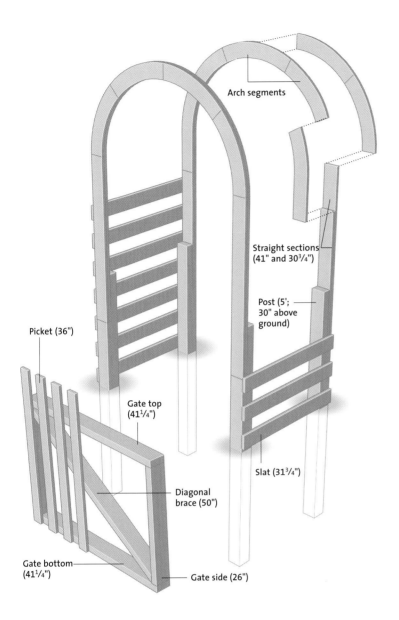

Arch segments

Straight sections
(41" and 30¾")

Post (5';
30" above
ground)

Picket (36")

Gate top
(41¼")

Slat (31¾")

Diagonal
brace (50")

Gate bottom
(41¼")

Gate side (26")

**1** **MAKE A PATTERN.** Start by laying out the curve of the arch on a piece of plywood or cardboard. You may want to paint the cardboard or plywood white to make it easy to see your lines. Mark the center along one edge and use a pencil tied to a piece of string to draw curves around that point. (Or use a trammel, as shown on pages 81 and 85.) The radius (the length of the string) is 21 inches for the inside curve and 24½ inches for the outside curve. Divide the arch into four equal sections by marking lines from the center at 45, 90, and 135 degrees, as shown.

**2** **CUT THE ARCH SEGMENTS.** On the pattern, measure the distance from where the center line intersects the inner curve to where one of the other two lines intersects the same curve. The distance should be about 16¹⁄₁₆ inches. Cut the arch segments to 21 inches. Set your power miter saw to cut a 22.5-degree angle and cut both ends of seven arch segments, making the pieces into trapezoids. The short side of each piece should equal the distance you measured between the points on the inner curve of the plywood. On two other pieces, cut only one end at an angle, locating the cut so that the long sides of these pieces match the long sides of the other pieces. Repeat the process to cut segments for the second arch.

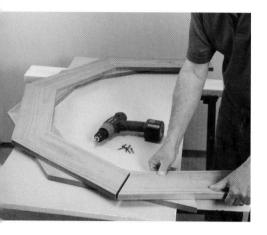

**3** **ASSEMBLE THE ARCH LAYERS.** For each arch, select four of the double-cut arch segments for the first layer. Measure and mark a center line across each piece. Tape a layer of waxed paper over the pattern to keep the arch from sticking to it. Swab exterior wood glue on the ends of the arch segments and set them in place over the pattern, marked side up. Add the other five segments as a second layer, coating the joining faces with glue and aligning the segment ends of the top layer with the center lines on the first layer. Start with the center piece and work your way out to the ends. The final segments will run past the ends of the first layer. Drill pilot holes and screw the pieces in place with 1¼-inch screws. Drive five screws per segment, two near each end and one in the center. Be sure to drive the heads just below the surface so you can fill the holes later.

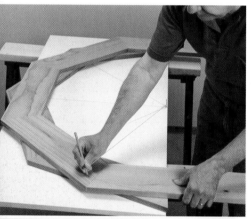

**4** **CUT THE ARCHES.** After the glue dries, draw the curves for the arch on each arch assembly, using a string and pencil as in Step 1. Keep the arch assembly in position on the pattern and use the same center point you used to make the original curves. Below the bottom edge of the pattern, extend the curve into straight lines where the arches will meet the straight leg sections. Cut out the arches with a jigsaw. Sand the sawed edges.

**5** **ADD THE STRAIGHT SECTIONS.** For each leg on each arch, measure how far the second layer extends past the first layer. Subtract this figure from 41 inches, then cut a piece of that length for the short straight section on that side. Cut two other pieces 41 inches long. Each arch should have two long straight pieces and two short ones (see diagram, page 109). Align the pieces, apply glue, and drive screws.

**BUILDING OPTION**

If it's more convenient, build the entire structure on a flat surface, then place it on the ground to mark for the postholes.

**6** **NOTCH THE POSTS.** The straight sections of the arches mate with notches in the ends of the 4 by 4 posts. First, cut each post to length. Then cut a notch 1½ inches deep and 12 inches long. Start with a circular saw, then finish the cuts with a handsaw.

**7** **SET POSTS AND ATTACH ARCHES.** Lay out for four posts so they will form a rectangle with inside dimensions of 42 inches by 23 inches. Dig 30-inch holes for the posts (see pages 154–156). Set the posts in place and check that the shoulders are level with each other; adjust hole depths as needed. Temporarily brace the posts. Glue and screw the arches to the posts with 2-inch screws.

**8** **PAINT, THEN ATTACH SLATS.** Cut the slats. Fill screw holes and prime and paint the structure and the slats. Starting at center top, drill pilot holes and fasten each slat to the arches with four 2-inch screws or power-driven nails. Space the slats about 4 inches apart, using two 4-inch spacers cut from scrap lumber. Fill the holes and apply one or two coats of paint.

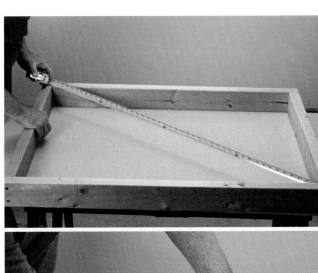

**9** **BUILD THE GATE FRAME.** The gate is a simple 2 by 4 frame with a diagonal brace and a series of pickets. Cut the top and bottom pieces ³/₄ inch shorter than the distance between the posts; hold them in place and test to see that there is enough clearance for the gate to swing. Cut the sides and screw the frame together with 4-inch screws. To make sure the frame is square, measure the diagonals. If the measurements are not equal, apply pressure across whichever diagonal is longer until the distances match up.

**10** **INSTALL THE BRACE.** With the frame squared, hold a 2 by 4 in place and mark it for cutting, as shown. Use a power miter saw to cut each end at an angle. Set the brace inside the gate frame and fasten it by drilling pilot holes and driving 2-inch screws.

**11** **ADD THE PICKETS.** Cut the pickets to length and cut the tops to match the rest of your fence. Prime and paint the pickets and the frame, then attach the pickets with 2-inch screws. Add hinges, hang the gate, and add a latch (see page 113).

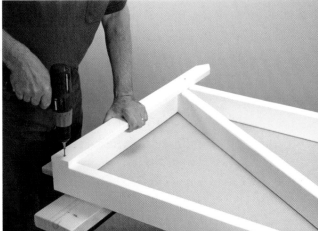

# Building a Gate

If your arbor will have a gate, build the arbor first, then make the gate to fit; setting posts in precise positions is difficult. For a basic gate with a Z-frame, see page 111. Here we start with that same Z-frame and add fencing boards with a curved top.

see page 111

## Gate Stops

Plan the direction your gate will swing, and also how it will stop. Here are the basic options. If you expect the gate to be slammed hard, the first option is preferred.

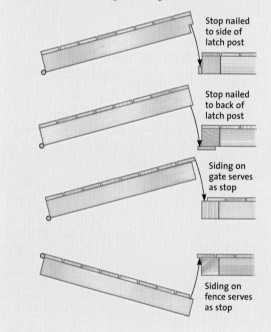

Stop nailed to side of latch post

Stop nailed to back of latch post

Siding on gate serves as stop

Siding on fence serves as stop

**2** **MARK A CURVED TOP.** To trace a smooth arc, make a guide with a nail and a piece of string. (You could also use a cardboard trammel, as shown on page 85.) Draw other types of shapes freehand or with the help of a framing square.

as shown on page 85

**3** **CUT THE CURVE.** Be sure there's no gate framing behind the cutting line, then cut the top using a jigsaw. Lightly sand the cut edges to make them less likely to splinter.

**1** **LAY OUT BOARDS.** Test-fit the siding boards and adjust as needed. You may choose to have gaps between the boards, but keep in mind that new lumber usually shrinks and produces ¹/₈-inch gaps anyway. Let the board tops run long and cut them later. Mark the siding boards with the positions of the framing pieces. Starting at the hinge side of the gate, drive nails or screws to attach the siding to the frame.

# Hanging a Gate

Position the gate so that it has at least 2 inches of clearance above the ground. If you expect heavy snow or lots of leaves, 4 to 6 inches is preferable. Choose hinges that take full advantage of your framing. These hinges have a leaf on one side to attach to the vertical post and a strap on the other to attach to the horizontal gate frame.

**1** **FASTEN HINGES TO THE GATE.** Position each hinge on the gate with its leaf hanging down as shown, and drill pilot holes through the hinge's screw holes. Screw the hinges to the gate frame.

**2** **PROP THE GATE IN THE OPENING.** Have a helper hold the gate in place, or prop it in position with wood blocks at the bottom and shims on each side. If the gap between the gate and the posts is more than a bit uneven (precision is usually not expected), plane or adjust the positions of siding pieces on the gate as needed.

**3** **SCREW HINGES TO THE POST.** Drill pilot holes, then drive screws into the post to attach the hinges. Remove the shims and test the swing. You may choose to add a return spring so that the gate closes automatically.

**4** **INSTALL A LATCH.** To install a self-closing latch, first drill pilot holes and drive screws to install the strike (the portion with no moving parts) onto the gate frame. Hold the latch in position, and test that the strike will slide into it easily. Mark its location and attach the latch with screws.

# ROUGH-HEWN ARBOR

THE CRISP EDGES AND STRAIGHT LINES OF LUMBERYARD MATERIALS LOOK GOOD IN MANY GARDENS, but the formality of 2-by and 4-by lumber may not be the look you want. Branches and logs, whether straight or curved, can increase your design options considerably—and often for very little cost. Rough-hewn structures are surprisingly well-suited to a number of yard settings. You may choose to assemble a grouping of rustic structures, perhaps including bentwood trellises like those shown on pages 50–52. Or, a single woody element can provide a nice contrast to a more formal setting.

## Getting Ready

Rustic materials add charm to any garden structure, but they may not last as long as pressure-treated lumber, or cedar or redwood. Depending on the species and weather conditions, the bark may fall off and reveal sound wood, or the branch may rot from within. For the longest-lasting structure, look for wood from trees that are naturally rot resistant, such as cedar, oak, or locust.

If you don't have access to a woodlot from which to cut your materials, check in with your local municipality or utility company to see if you can follow one of their tree crews to collect the trimmings.

As a general rule, gather about 50 percent more than you think you need; often, branches look less straight or attractive once you have trimmed them.

## Materials List

- Logs, 4" to 8" in diameter, for posts
- Branches about 3" in diameter for cross braces
- Branches about 1" to 2" in diameter for lattice pieces
- Weathered lattice sections (optional, see photo)
- 8" or 12" galvanized barn spikes
- 3" and 4" decking screws

## SAFETY TIP

Use a gas-powered chain saw only if you have experience using one. This tool is so powerful that even a momentary lapse in judgment can lead to serious harm. Always position yourself so that if the saw slips or kicks back it will not touch you. The electric chain saw shown here is less powerful, but still dangerous. You can make most if not all of these cuts using a reciprocating saw equipped with a landscaping blade; the work will be considerably slower—and considerably less dangerous.

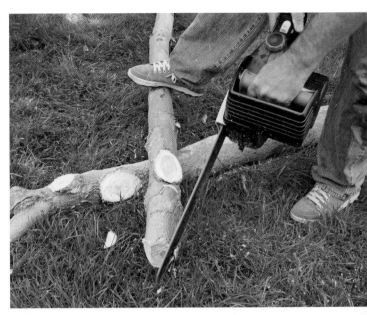

**1** **TRIM LOGS AND LARGE BRANCHES.**
Keeping your legs well away from the potential path of the saw blade, cut off branches that will not be part of the arbor. Cut them so they are basically flush with the plane of the log, as shown, or, for a more woodsy look, allow some branches to poke out several inches.

**2** **PREPARE AN END FOR JOINING.** To achieve the look of joinery, cut a partial point in the end of a cross brace to be joined to a post. (See Step 5 for the final joint.)

**3** **MARK THE POST FOR A NOTCH.** Hold the cross brace in place against the log and use a handsaw to mark for the notch.

**4** **CUT AND CHISEL A NOTCH.** Use a chain saw or a reciprocating saw to cut at angles into the post, then chisel out the notch. Test the fit. You will probably need to modify the notch or the cross brace's cut end to achieve a tight joint.

**5** **DRILL PILOT HOLES.** You could attach a massive joint like this simply by driving a spike or two, but it's well worth the trouble to drill pilot holes for the spikes first. Drill through the post, but not through the cross brace; the spike will travel more easily along the length of a branch than across the grain of the post. Two spikes, driven at different angles, will make for a long-lasting joint.

**6** **DRIVE THE SPIKES.** Use a small sledge-hammer to drive spikes through the pilot holes and into the cross braces. Follow the same steps at each joint.

**PRO TIP**

In most cases, cutting and joining will be easier and more accurate if you place small branch scraps under the pieces to raise them off the ground as you work.

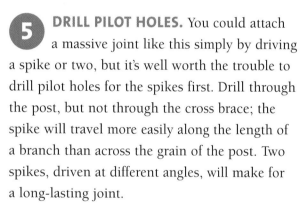

**7** **PREPARE ANGLED BRACES.** Cut angled braces at about 45 degrees on each end. Test the fit, and recut either end as needed to produce a tight joint. Drill pilot holes through each brace.

**8** **ATTACH BRACES.** Use screws to attach the angled braces. You could drive smaller spikes, but 3- or 4-inch screws hold better and are virtually invisible once their heads are driven partway into the brace.

**9** **ANCHOR THE POSTS.** A log that is set in a posthole may rot quickly. Instead, you can sprinkle and tamp some gravel onto the ground, set the post on the gravel, drill a steeply angled pilot hole, and drive a spike into the ground. For greater support, drill a thicker pilot hole and drive lengths of ³/₈-inch rebar. Once the arbor frame is in place, add slats, lattice, or rafters to taste. You can use more branches, or substitute weathered lumber.

## Working with Rustic Materials

Building with rustic materials often requires a different mindset than working with traditional lumber. You'll need to be a little more flexible in terms of size, relative straightness, and even the way you measure. If a piece tapers, take this into consideration when laying out or cutting a joint. Keep the overall picture in mind rather than getting bogged down with individual measurements that may not add up perfectly.

Still, you don't need to strive for an imperfect, rustic effect; that will come of its own accord. Aim for accuracy and symmetry as much as possible, and you'll like the final results.

# choosing
## the right
# plants

A FRESHLY BUILT TRELLIS OR ARBOR IS ONLY
HALF FINISHED UNTIL A VINE OR TWO CLIMBS
ONTO IT. THIS CHAPTER HELPS YOU CHOOSE
PLANTS THAT WILL PROSPER IN YOUR CLIMATE
AND MICROCLIMATE AND SHOWS HOW TO
CULTIVATE AND TRAIN THEM.

# ALL ABOUT VINES

YOUR TASTE WILL GUIDE YOU in choosing the best adornment for your trellis or arbor. (Alternatively, you can choose the plant first and then design your structure to match it.) But before making your selection, consider the following key issues. Then consult pages 125–135 for information on many popular vines, including some annual possibilities and roses. Pages 122–124 show techniques for cultivating, pruning, and training.

## Prime Considerations

Start by selecting a plant that suits your structure in general scale. For a large arbor, look for a big, fast-growing vine that will provide the coverage you want. Certain heavy plants, including most climbing roses, should only be used with large, sturdy structures. For a modest trellis, select a vine with smaller features.

Choose a vine suited to your climate and microclimate (the conditions at a particular place on your property). If the plant will grow in a spot in the yard that gets only dappled sunlight, for instance, a plant that needs full sunlight may send out only a few flowers; you may be better off with a vine that emphasizes its leaves. Consult the staff of the gardening department or nursery where you buy your vine. Keep in mind that plants grow toward the light and flower on one side only, so position the plant to best advantage. Also consider that walls and fences create a rain shadow. Plants should be at least a yard away from them so they'll get their fair share of rain. Keep a file of the care requirements of the plants you select so you can prune and train them later in the season to achieve the best results.

Also consider which climbers your arbor or trellis can handle best. Does the structure provide the right footholds for tendrils or twining, or will you need to help plants to hold on, using the techniques shown on page 123?

BELOW LEFT: **Clematis and roses are ideal climbing companions, as their soil, nutrient, and watering needs are essentially the same.** BELOW RIGHT: *Lathyrus odoratus* **(sweet pea) is a delicate twining vine that prefers more slender supports, like this willow trellis.**

# How Vines Climb

To know what sort of structure a vine can scale, you need to know just how it climbs. If necessary, you can accommodate the structure to the vine—for example, by adding vertical wires against the sides of an arbor post to support twining or coiling vines.

**Twining.** Vines such as honeysuckle (*Lonicera*) send out stems that will coil around anything slender, growing upward in the process. In nature, they often wrap around the branches of other plants, which then in effect become living trellises. Twining vines can wrap around thin lattice slats, dowels, wire, or string; they will need to be tied to a 4 by 4 or a 2 by 4, and may even need help holding onto a 1 by 2.

Twining stem

Coiling tendril

**Coiling.** Vines like grape (*Vitis*) and sweet pea (*Lathyrus odoratus*) have specialized growths that will wrap around anything handy. Usually forked or branched, these tendrils either arise from the stem or form part of the leaves. In some vines, such as cat's claw (*Macfadyena unguis-cati*), the tendrils have the ability to hook onto rough surfaces. A few vines, like clematis, have coiling leafstalks that behave like tendrils. Coiling vines need fairly slender vertical supports: wire, rope, rods, or narrow lattice slats. They will also attach to horizontal supports, spreading sideways as well as upward.

Clinging aerial rootlets

Clinging holdfast disc

**Clinging.** Clinging vines like ivy (*Hedera*) look terrific on solid masonry, but may not be suited to your trellis or arbor. You can't easily guide their growth because they have specialized stem growths such as holdfast (suction) discs and aerial rootlets that attach firmly to all but slick surfaces. These vines can usually grab onto 2 by 4s and larger boards, as long as the boards are not coated with a high-gloss paint. Thinning and pruning require physically detaching the vines, and the typical dense growth obscures the support structure.

No means of attachment

**Clambering.** Clambering plants have long, flexible stems with no means of attachment, though some have thorns that help them hook their way through other plants. These vines must be tied to their supports, with new ties added as they grow and spread. Climbing roses and bougainvillea are familiar clambering vines.

# Planting

Check the instructions that come with the plant for recommended planting times. Where winters are mild, it's generally best to plant during winter; this gives time for the roots to establish themselves before warm weather sets in and the growing season begins. In regions with cold winters, plant as early in spring as you can to give the vine as long an establishment period as possible. Plants set out in warmer weather endure heat stress while trying to establish themselves, and so put out less growth. Since plants need air circulation, keep trellises a few inches away from a nearby wall or fence.

**1  DIG AND PLANT.** Prepare the soil by removing weeds and digging in some coarse organic material such as compost, sawdust, manure, leaf mold, or peat to improve the soil's texture and increase water retention. Dig a hole at least twice the diameter of the container the plant comes in, so the roots will have plenty of room to spread. Before removing the plant, water it well, then let it drain for an hour. Slide the plant out and gently uncurl the roots. Remove any dead or damaged roots by cutting them back close to the rootball. Position the plant in the hole, angled toward the trellis, with the top of the rootball level with the soil.

**2  PRUNE.** Nip off any wilted ends or flowers that have started to fade. Some experts recommend cutting off even healthy-looking blooms, to encourage the growth of new ones. Fan out the plant's main shoots and tie them individually to the support, as described on the next page.

**3  WATER AND MULCH.** Press down around the perimeter of the hole to form a sort of moat, so water can pool there rather than flowing away from the plant. Water generously. Cover with a layer of mulch to inhibit weed growth and to help hold in moisture.

## Supporting

During the first several years of a typical vine's life, you'll need to guide its stems, perhaps starting with angled supports to lead them to the arbor or trellis. For vines that twine or coil, be on the lookout for tangles. If the stems wrap around or cling to each other, untwine them or detach the stems. For a clambering vine with no means of attachment, tie the stems to the trellis or arbor as they lengthen.

Some vines become heavy as they grow; others send out lightweight shoots that are easily windblown. Either way, most vines need some sort of support. See page 121 for the various ways in which vines grab onto trellises and arbors.

Gardeners use all sorts of things for tying up vines, including rags, strips of panty hose, and twine. Perhaps the safest choice is a flexible green plastic tape made for the purpose (right, top). Even if you tie fairly tightly, the tape will flex to allow the vine unimpeded growth. Plant ties made of metal wire coated with a colored plastic strip (right, middle) are the easiest to attach, but

if they are tied tightly, they may cut a vine as it grows. Either tie loosely, or check them every month or so to see if they need to be adjusted. For strong, thick vines, a series of wires may be used for guides (left). Make sure the plants can wrap themselves around the wire and not vice versa. See pages 40–41 for more information.

Some vines wrap themselves gracefully around a thick post, but others need to be tied. Use a strong but flexible tie (left). If you have lattice with closely spaced slats, you may not need any ties. Every couple of weeks, gently interlace the vine through the lattice (right, bottom).

The point of pruning is to encourage new growth, help shape the plant, and keep it healthy. A sharp pair of hand pruners makes a clean cut, and creates a wound that quickly heals. Generally, it's best to cut a quarter or half inch above a bud and to cut at a 45-degree angle.

## Pruning and Thinning

Pruning needs vary with a plant's age, health, and vigor—and where it is growing. For example, an exuberant, fast-growing wisteria must be pruned heavily if it's attached to a modest structure. A slow-growing plant attached to a large arbor may never need to be pruned.

For a new vine, remove growth that competes with the main structure of the plant, or errant growth that cannot be guided back into place. For a mature plant, most pruning involves removing dead or weak stems and thinning excess growth, sometimes to untangle the plant, and other times to reveal more of the trellis or arbor.

## Feeding and Watering

Even if a plant is growing too quickly for your taste, don't neglect regular feeding, using a fertilizer recommended for the plant. An underfed flowering plant may have fewer blooms than usual, and the blooms may be small or short-lived. Most vines need lots of regular watering the first year, and a bit less in following years. New or small plants have shallow roots and require frequent but small amounts of water. Established plants with deep roots need ample amounts of water—perhaps provided by allowing a hose to trickle for a half hour—several times a season.

# TOP 40 PLANT PICKS

THE PLANT WORLD OFFERS A VAST VARIETY of climbing vines for your trellis or arbor. Here we present a brief guide to some favorites, many of which are available in numerous colors and varieties. Use it to assemble a list of promising options. Then check at your local garden department or nursery for those best suited to your climate and region.

*Actinidia kolomikta 'Arctic Beauty'*

## Actinidia
#### Kiwi vine

**Style:** Twining. **Characteristics:** Tolerates some shade; *A. deliciosa* bears fruit (kiwi); deciduous. **Special notes:** Requires strong support; depending on species, good for arbors, screens, wall trellises, or fencetop or walltop trellises.

## Akebia quinata
#### Fiveleaf akebia

**Style:** Twining. **Characteristics:** Fast growing; tolerates some shade; showy flowers in spring; decorative fruit; deciduous to evergreen. **Special notes:** Creates a mass foliage effect; good for arbors or as backdrop on large wall trellises.

## Ampelopsis brevipedunculata
#### Porcelain berry

**Style:** Coiling (tendrils). **Characteristics:** Fast growing; tolerates some shade; needs only moderate water; decorative fruit; deciduous. **Special notes:** Grapelike, heavy; best on sturdy arbors.

## Aristolochia macrophylla
#### Dutchman's pipe

**Style:** Twining. **Characteristics:** Fast growing; tolerates some shade; deciduous. **Special notes:** Traditional favorite for thick cover on trellises, screens, fences; avoid in windy areas.

*Ampelopsis brevipedunculata*

## Beaumontia grandiflora
#### Easter lily vine

**Style:** Somewhat twining. **Characteristics:** Tolerates some shade; fragrant; showy flowers in spring and summer; evergreen. **Special notes:** Requires tying when young; needs sturdy support; use on arbors and very large trellises.

*Campsis radicans*

## Bougainvillea

**Style:** Clambering; must be tied. **Characteristics:** Showy flowers in spring, summer, and fall; evergreen. **Special notes:** Use in mild climates on screens, fences, or large arbors.

## Campsis
### Trumpet vine

**Style:** Clinging. **Characteristics:** Tolerates partial shade; several varieties with large funnel-shaped flowers that appear in late summer; deciduous. **Special notes:** Fairly robust plant, needs a strong structure.

*Clerodendrum thomsoniae*

*Clytostoma callistegioides*

## Clematis

**Style:** Coiling (leafstalks). **Characteristics:** Tolerates some shade; showy flowers in spring, summer, or fall; mostly deciduous. **Special notes:** Many varieties; better for trellises than arbors. Plant two or three varieties in a single location for blooms that occur at different times.

## Clerodendrum thomsoniae
### Bleeding heart glorybower

**Style:** Twining. **Characteristics:** Tolerates some shade; showy flowers in summer; evergreen. **Special notes:** In warm climates, grow on trellises or posts; in cool climates, use with portable (container) trellises.

## Clytostoma callistegioides
### Violet trumpet vine

**Style:** Coiling (tendrils on leaves). **Characteristics:** Fast growing; tolerates some shade; needs only moderate water; showy flowers in spring and summer; evergreen. **Special notes:** On arbors, grows long, trailing streamers; on wire trellises, forms solid mass.

# Quick Picks

**PLANTS FOR SHADY (OR PARTLY SHADY) SITES**
Clematis
Climbing hydrangea
Ivy
Winter jasmine
Some varieties of roses

**FAST GROWERS**
Clematis
Honeysuckle
Russian vine
Virginia creeper
Grapevines
Annuals such as morning glory, sweet peas, and climbing nasturtiums

**FRAGRANT PLANTS**
Climbing roses
Honeysuckle
Sweet peas
Wisteria

*Clematis 'General Sikorski'*

*× Fatshedera lizei*

## Distictis
##### Mexican blood flower or blood trumpet

**Style:** Coiling (tendrils). **Characteristics:** Fast growing; tolerates some shade; fragrant, showy flowers in spring, summer, and fall; evergreen. **Special notes:** Use on arbors, large wall trellises, or fencetop or walltop trellises.

## Fallopia

**Style:** Twining. **Characteristics:** Fast growing, rugged; needs only moderate water; showy flowers in spring, summer, and fall; evergreen to deciduous. **Special notes:** Popular in seaside or arid zones; also use on trellises to conceal ugly features.

## × Fatshedera lizei

**Style:** Clambering; must be tied. **Characteristics:** Tolerates some shade; evergreen. **Special notes:** Cross of English ivy and Japanese aralia; does not cling; suitable for trellises.

## Ficus pumila
##### Creeping fig or climbing fig

**Style:** Clinging. **Characteristics:** Half-hardy plant that is perennial only in mild climates; distinctive shiny leaves in shades of green and yellow. **Special notes:** Young stems have clinging holdfasts, but mature branches may need support; will grow vigorously in sun.

## Gelsemium sempervirens
##### Carolina jessamine

**Style:** Twining. **Characteristics:** Tolerates some shade; fragrant, showy flowers in midwinter and early spring; evergreen. **Special notes:** All parts are toxic if ingested; climbs well on trellises with wires; grows delicate trailing streamers on arbors.

## Hardenbergia

**Style:** Twining. **Characteristics:** Tolerates some shade; showy flowers in winter and spring; evergreen. **Special notes:** Modest in size; suited to posts, wall trellises, fencetop and walltop trellises, and small arbors.

*Gelsemium sempervirens*

## Hibbertia scandens
##### Guinea gold vine

**Style:** Twining. **Characteristics:** Tolerates some shade; long-blooming, showy flowers in spring, summer, and fall; evergreen. **Special notes:** Popular in mild-winter climates; use on pillars, trellises, and small arbors.

*Hardenbergia*

## Humulus lupulus
### Common hop

**Style:** Twining. **Characteristics:** Very fast growing; beautiful foliage, with two colors of flower followed by the hops themselves; deciduous. **Special notes:** All stems die after frost—remove before spring to allow for new ones.

## Hydrangea petiolaris
### Climbing hydrangea

**Style:** Clinging. **Characteristics:** Tolerates partial shade; needs frequent watering; two types of flowers appear abundantly over much of the summer; deciduous. **Special notes:** Vigorously climbing shrub, needs a sturdy structure.

*Hydrangea petiolaris*

*Humulus lupulus 'Aureus'*

## Jasminum
### Jasmine

**Style:** Twining. **Characteristics:** Tolerates some shade; fragrant, showy flowers in winter, spring, or summer; evergreen, semi-evergreen, or deciduous. **Special notes:** Many species; easy to grow; produces delicate abundance of foliage on arbors, solid mass on trellises.

## Lapageria rosea
### Chilean bellflower

**Style:** Twining. **Characteristics:** Tolerates some shade; very showy flowers in spring, summer, and fall; evergreen. **Special notes:** Strikingly elegant; requires sheltered location, well-drained soil amended with organic matter; use on trellises or posts.

*Jasminum polyanthum*

## Ipomoea
### Morning glory

**Style:** Twining. **Characteristics:** Many types require a sunny spot that is at least partly sheltered from strong winds; vigorous, woody plant with trumpet-shaped flowers that appear at various times depending on the species. **Special notes:** Hundreds of species available; a perennial in warm climates and an annual elsewhere (see page 130).

*Ipomoea (Convolvulus 'Star of Yelta')*

## Lathyrus latifolius
### Perennial sweet pea

**Style:** Clambering. **Characteristics:** Hardy and vigorous, growing well in cold climates and tolerating poor soil; wing-shaped leaves; flowers, which range from violet to red, appear in late spring or early summer. **Special notes:** Though easy to grow, it does need to be tied—perhaps several times a season—because it grows quickly.

*Lonicera sempervirens*

*Pandorea*

## Macfadyena unguis-cati
#### Cat's claw or yellow trumpet vine

**Style:** Coiling (tendrils). **Characteristics:** Fast growing; tolerates some shade; needs only moderate water; showy flowers in spring; evergreen to deciduous. **Special notes:** Use to cover patio overheads quickly.

## Mandevilla

**Style:** Twining. **Characteristics:** Tolerates some shade; fragrant, showy flowers in any season, depending on variety; evergreen, semievergreen, or deciduous. **Special notes:** Requires well-drained, organically enriched soil; *M. laxa* is best for arbors and large trellises, other species for trellises or pillars.

## Pandorea

**Style:** Twining. **Characteristics:** Tolerates some shade; needs only moderate water; showy flowers in spring, summer, and fall; evergreen. **Special notes:** Look for *P. jasminoides* or *P. pandorana*.

## Lonicera
#### Honeysuckle

**Style:** Twining. **Characteristics:** Fast growing; tolerates some shade; needs only moderate water; fragrant, showy flowers in spring, summer, and fall; evergreen, semievergreen, or deciduous. **Special notes:** Most varieties best suited to large arbors; smaller species can be used on trellises and pillars.

*Mandevilla × amabilis* 'Alice du Pont'

# The Annual Alternative

Most trellises and arbors are filled with long-lived plants that flourish and mature for years. But there are times when an annual vine is a better choice. You can use an annual to fill in empty spaces on a new trellis or arbor, or to cover up bare stems at the base of an older one. In regions with harsh winters, annual vines provide rich abundance in the warm months without creating unwelcome shade in winter. And annuals offer the opportunity to bring new life to your trellis or arbor year after year, so you can enjoy an ever-changing display of blooms.

Certain annual vines are longtime favorites in country or cottage gardens for their abundant color and rapid growth. Gourd vines work well on trellises, as do black-eyed Susan vine *(Thunbergia alata)*, orange clock vine *(Thunbergia gregorii)*, sweet pea *(Lathyrus odoratus)*, and nasturtium *(Tropaeolum majus)*—a favorite for children to plant, with its large seeds, fast growth, and bright flowers. For small arbors, consider the vigorous cup-and-saucer vine *(Cobaea scandens)* or one of the many varieties of morning glory *(Ipomoea)*.

Left: *Tropaeolum majus*. Top: *Cobaea scandens*. Bottom: *Thunbergia alata* 'Suzie'. Right: Gourds.

*Parthenocissus quinquefolia*

## Parthenocissus
### Virginia creeper, Boston ivy, and others

**Style:** Coiling (tendrils); sometimes clinging. **Characteristics:** Most types are slow growing; woody plants with negligible flowers but showy leaves; leaves turn reddish brown in fall, then drop off in winter; some types have berries. **Special notes:** There is a debate as to whether ivy damages house siding or masonry, but it is a good choice if you want a blanketlike covering for a trellis or arbor. Leaves are dense and may hide the wooden members of the structure.

## Passiflora
### Passion vine

**Style:** Coiling (tendrils). **Characteristics:** Fast growing; tolerates some shade; needs only moderate water; showy flowers in spring, summer, or fall; decorative fruit; evergreen, semievergreen, or deciduous. **Special notes:** Best suited to large arbors; on large trellises, prune and thin often.

## Podranea ricasoliana
### Pink trumpet vine

**Style:** Twining. **Characteristics:** Moderate growth; tolerates some shade; needs only moderate water; showy flowers in summer; evergreen to deciduous. **Special notes:** A refined accent on pillars, small arbors, or trellises.

## Pyrostegia venusta
### Flame vine

**Style:** Twining and coiling (tendrils). **Characteristics:** Fast growing; needs only moderate water; showy flowers in fall, winter, and spring; decorative fruit; evergreen. **Special notes:** Well suited to large trellises or arbors.

## Rubus occidentalis
### Black or red raspberry

**Style:** Clambering. **Characteristics:** Vigorous, even invasive plant with sharp thorns and fruit that ranges from sour to sweet; many types produce fruit through most of the growing season. **Special notes:** Once established, needs to be cut back annually to prevent it from taking over; a trellis offers a good way to get at the fruits without having to push through a tangle of thorny branches.

## Solandra maxima
### Cup-of-gold vine

**Style:** Clambering; must be tied. **Characteristics:** Fast growing; showy flowers in winter and spring; evergreen. **Special notes:** Requires shelter from frost and wind; showcase it on arbors, large trellises, or walltop trellises.

*Passiflora*

Solanum

## Solanum
### Includes potato vine, Costa Rican nightshade, Brazilian nightshade

**Style:** Twining, coiling, or clambering. **Characteristics:** Showy flowers in spring or summer; other characteristics vary by species; evergreen to deciduous. **Special notes:** Easy to grow; requires mild climate; most varieties suited to trellises and pillars, large varieties better for arbors.

Stephanotis floribunda

## Stephanotis floribunda
### Madagascar jasmine

**Style:** Twining. **Characteristics:** Tolerates some shade; fragrant, showy flowers in spring and summer; evergreen. **Special notes:** In frost-free zones, use on obelisks, small arbors, or trellises; in cooler areas, use with portable (container) trellises.

## Tecoma capensis
### Cape honeysuckle

**Style:** Clambering; must be tied. **Characteristics:** Needs only moderate water; showy flowers in summer, fall, and winter; evergreen. **Special notes:** Tolerates hot summers well; suited to both trellises and arbors.

## Trachelospermum jasminoides
### Star jasmine

**Style:** Twining. **Characteristics:** Tolerates some shade; fragrant, showy flowers in spring and summer; evergreen. **Special notes:** Excellent year-round for trellises in prominent garden spots; also use on small arbors or pillars.

## Tropaeolum majus
### Nasturtium

**Style:** Twining. **Characteristics:** Tolerates some shade; vigorous woody plant with showy flowers; species offer varied flower colors and different shapes for both flowers and leaves. **Special notes:** Dense, large leaves provide good shade for an arbor.

## Vitis
### Grape

**Style:** Coiling (tendrils). **Characteristics:** Fast growing; needs only moderate water; decorative fruit (grapes); deciduous. **Special notes:** Varieties include table, wine, and ornamental grapes; best on large arbors.

Vitis

## Wisteria

**Style:** Twining. **Characteristics:** Fast growing; tolerates some shade; needs only moderate water; fragrant, showy flowers in winter, spring, and summer; deciduous. **Special notes:** Very heavy, requires strong support; a showpiece for large arbors; can grow on large, securely attached trellises.

Wisteria

# ROSES

ROSES ARE OFTEN THE CROWNING GLORY OF A GARDEN, and a particularly lovely plant may be the envy of the neighborhood. Roses have a reputation for being fussy, but in fact they are like most other plants. They need sunshine and water. They are fussy to the extent that they like quite a lot of both. They also like good drainage, which can usually be supplied by digging in lots of compost. Adding a nitrogen-rich fertilizer is helpful, too. Because they have thorns, roses should be positioned out of traffic. The thorns may also have the benefit of keeping children from climbing onto a fragile trellis.

**The large-blossomed 'Constance Spry' is a disease-resistant rose that flowers in the spring. It can grow to 15 feet when trained as a climber.**

## Choosing Your Roses

Climbing roses are an investment that usually takes several years to reach maturity, so take your time to choose the best variety to succeed in your garden.

Compared with bush roses, climbing roses have longer and stronger canes and can grow upward on a structure with a little assistance. They have no natural means of attaching to a structure, and will simply trail on the ground unless trained and tied. There are two basic types of climbing roses: ramblers and climbers. Ramblers have

shorter canes and often blossom the first year. They produce massive floral displays that usually appear in one big flush in spring. Climbers have longer canes and generally do not bloom until they are at least a year old, but they tend to bloom all season long. Some shrub roses and miniature roses (the "tall" ones) can also be trained to climb.

Roses classified as climbers vary in height at maturity from 6 to 30 feet. Ramblers, the most vigorous climbing roses, will cover a house roof. More moderate climbers are better choices for arbors and tall, sturdy trellises. Smaller climbers are suitable for a trellis.

Most roses need full sun to bloom and stay disease-free, but a few varieties thrive in partial shade. Lighter-colored roses (for example, pale yellow or pink) tend to tolerate shade better, while darker shades (like deep red or orange) generally need more sun; a rose that needs a lot of sun may refuse to bloom in the wrong site.

There are literally thousands of rose varieties, with hundreds more being developed every year. (Many are named after the amateur breeder's spouse, child, or hero.) These pages show only a few of the more popular varieties.

'Moonlight', a hybrid musk rose, climbs a weathered arbor set among a bed of *Iris germanica*.

## Training and Maintaining Roses

It's best to install your arbor or trellis before you plant your roses. For planting, see pages 122–124 for general tips. For climbing roses, the planting hole should be 1½ feet away from the arbor or post. Set the plant in the hole at a 45-degree angle, so the canes lean toward the support.

Use temporary stakes to support canes that are too short to reach a trellis or arbor. Push the stakes into the soil at the base of the plant and secure them to the trellis. Then tie the canes to the stakes.

Once the plant is established, tie the stiffer canes to your arbor or trellis structure and splay the more limber canes outward to encourage side-to-side growth and more blooms. You may need to wait a year before the canes are long enough for training. Use a flexible material like gardening tape to secure the canes to the structure. If you're training a rose on a lattice, you may only need to thread the canes through the openings to shape the plant.

For the first two years, a new rose plant should be watered deeply and regularly. Twice a year, add an infusion of plant food if it's recommended by the garden shop where you purchased your plant. Regularly remove any dead or damaged canes. In cold climates, some roses should be covered with special foam-plastic covers.

# Getting Rose Advice

Read up on your particular rose for specific instructions on watering, pruning, and winter care. The American Rose Society is an excellent resource. Its website (www.ars.org) has contact information for local rose societies and lists members who are willing to answer questions by email or phone about roses specific to the area. The website also has a library of rose care articles. See also Sunset's *Roses,* which is endorsed by the American Rose Society.

CLOCKWISE, FROM TOP LEFT: Disease-resistant 'John Cabot' stands up to cold weather; a great rose for cutting, 'Polka' thrives in mild climates; the velvety red, single-flowered 'Altissimo' is well-suited to foggy or cold regions; *Rosa wichuraiana* hybrid flowers during the spring; heat-tolerant 'Cécile Brünner' sits pretty in pale pink.

# tools

# materials and

# techniques

BUILDING A TRELLIS OR ARBOR SHOULD BE AN ENJOYABLE
EXPERIENCE. MANY PROJECTS CAN BE COMPLETED IN A DAY
OR LESS, AND WORKING OUTSIDE WILL NOT DISRUPT FAMILY
LIFE. THE JOB WILL PROCEED SMOOTHLY IF YOU HAVE ALL
THE NEEDED TOOLS ON HAND AND CAREFULLY CHOOSE YOUR
MATERIALS. YOU MAY EVEN USE THE PROJECT AS AN EXCUSE
TO BUY THAT TOOL YOU'VE BEEN LUSTING AFTER!

# THE RIGHT LUMBER

SINCE MOST TRELLIS AND ARBOR PROJECTS ARE SMALL, it may not cost much more to buy the best lumber available—adding to the structure's sturdiness and lifespan. Choose a type of lumber that has a proven record of survival in your climate. You may opt to keep it well-sealed with paint or finish or to leave it unfinished to "go gray" (see pages 157–158). Untreated pine, fir, or hemlock can be used for outside projects, but will rot quickly unless completely sealed with paint; the woods shown on these pages offer various degrees of protection against rot.

## Cedar and Redwood

Cedar has pleasing tones and texture, is easy to work with, and resists cracking and warping. However, only the dark-colored heartwood is resistant to rot; the lighter-colored sapwood will probably rot in a few years unless you live in a very dry climate. Plan to keep it well sealed. Cedar is fairly soft, so it will likely become dented if children play on it.

Redwood has a distinctive beauty and is even more stable than cedar. Left unstained, it will acquire a silvery patina. However, redwood is expensive and difficult to find in many areas. As with cedar, only the dark heartwood is resistant to rot.

This fence/arbor employs clear lumber and furniture-like joinery for the fence slats and the trim pieces; the posts and overhead pieces are more knotty and rustic.

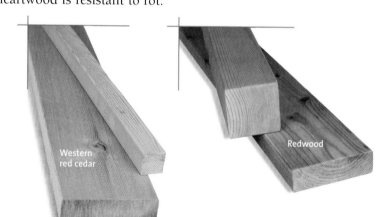

Western red cedar

Redwood

## Tropical Hardwoods

In addition to the more familiar mahogany and teak, rainforest "iron-woods" such as ipé, cambara, and meranti offer tremendous strength, stability, and resistance to rot. Boards are often perfectly straight, with close grain and few knots. Some types are so full of natural oil that they will not accept stain for a year or more; it is common to leave them unstained and allow them to turn a silvery gray. However, hardwoods are expensive and difficult to work with. You may need to drill pilot holes before driving each fastener.

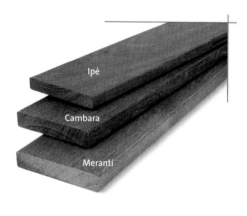

Ipé

Cambara

Meranti

## Pressure-Treated Lumber

Wood that has been factory-treated with preservatives is reliably long-lived even in harsh climates. However, all treated lumber is not the same.

**Treatment types and levels.** The plastic tags stapled to the ends of treated boards tell you the type of chemical used in the treatment, proper uses for the wood (including whether it is rated for ground contact), the initials of the testing agency (AWPA or ALSC, for American Wood Preservers' Association or American Lumber Standard Committee), and the name of the treatment company.

Older treated wood was infused with chromated copper arsenate (CCA), which has been banned for most residential use due to health concerns. Modern treatments include ammoniacal copper quaternary (ACQ), copper azole (CA), and copper borate azole (CBA, or CA-B).

All of these have been proved effective at resisting rot. However, many boards are rated "above ground," meaning they may rot if they contact the ground or remain wet for prolonged periods. For posts that will be sunk in the ground or placed where water may pool or collect, use lumber rated "ground contact."

**Fasteners.** The copper content of new treated lumber is corrosive to steel, which means that most galvanized nails, screws, or other hardware would deteriorate quickly. Check your fasteners to see that they are compatible with your lumber's treatment. Stainless-steel screws and nails are certain not to corrode.

Treated Douglas fir, stained

**Wood species.** Treated Douglas fir is strong and stable, but is sometimes difficult to find. Because fir does not readily accept treatment, it often has a grid of slits incised during the treatment process. These slits will still be visible when the wood is painted, so Douglas fir may not be a good choice for a structure that will be closely viewed.

Southern pine is also strong, but is often more prone to cracking and splitting than fir. Because it readily soaks up treatment, there are no incisions.

Treated Southern pine

**Finishing treated wood.** Most treated lumber has a greenish or yellowish color, which will fade in time to gray. You can buy stains designed to beautify green or graying treated lumber. You may need to wait a month or more for the treated wood to dry completely before applying finishes. If you want to paint your project right away (or paint the pieces before assembling them), pay a bit more for lumber labeled KDAT (kiln-dried after treatment) or S-Dry.

Composite hardwood

Composite hardwood

Composite softwood

## Synthetic Lumber

Though it is mostly made for use as decking or deck railings, some synthetic lumber may be appropriate for an arbor or trellis project. Composite lumber is made from wood fibers and other ingredients, while vinyl "lumber" is completely synthetic. Though expensive, synthetics are impervious to rot and will not split. They can be cut and attached much like standard lumber.

Synthetic boards are not very rigid, so they usually cannot be used as posts, beams, or rafters on a large structure. They also need to be supported at fairly close intervals or they will bend and warp. Some types swell, so abutting boards should be spaced at least $\frac{1}{8}$ inch apart. Some synthetics fade in color when exposed to the sun. Some can be painted, while others cannot.

## Trellis Panels

At a home center or lumberyard, you will likely find a variety of trellis panels, usually 4 feet by 8 feet. Using the panels can greatly speed up the building process, but may limit your design choices.

Natural wood panels may be made of pressure-treated wood or untreated fir or cedar slats. Choose panels that have a total thickness of at least $\frac{3}{4}$ inch (meaning that the individual slats are $\frac{3}{8}$ inch thick). Check that the slats are firmly attached together, and watch for splits, knots, and wane. Unless you want the trellis to turn gray, plan to paint wood lattice using a sprayer; painting with a brush will take much longer.

In addition to standard panels, which typically have evenly spaced $1\frac{1}{4}$-inch-wide slats, you can also purchase high-end panels in a greater variety of styles. These may be pricey. If your local supplier does not carry what you want, check online sources.

Vinyl panels will last forever and never need painting. However, they generally limit your color choices to white, and you will need to paint the other parts of the structure—making sure to match (or contrast with) the white of the vinyl so neither component looks dingy.

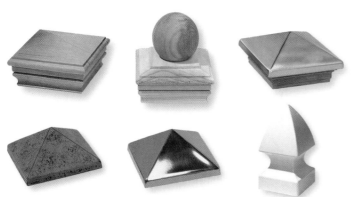

Vinyl panels are less rigid than wood, so you will have to support them at fairly close intervals.

## Post Caps

Decorate post tops with post caps, also called newels. A wide variety of styles and materials can be found at home centers, deck suppliers, and online.

## Selecting Boards

Trellises and arbors come in for close scrutiny, so take the time to examine each board to make sure it is straight and free of any of the unsightly defects shown at right. First check the board's surfaces, then raise one end and look down its length to make sure it's straight.

**Lumber grades.** A stamp or sticker on a board gives important details about the board's quality. Standard and No. 2 boards are strong enough, but boards rated Select or No. 1 are worth the extra cost. Cedar and redwood are graded for appearance and heartwood content. Choose boards with the word "heart" in the label, or look for dark-colored heartwood.

**Wet or dry treated wood?** Treated wood that is still wet from treatment will need to wait for a couple weeks or so before you can paint or stain it, but it tends to be straighter and freer of cracks than wood that has dried in the lumberyard. A board that is both dry and straight can be painted or stained very soon.

## Common defects

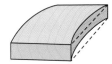

**CROOK.** A severe warp along the edge line. If the warp is greater than an inch in an 8-foot piece, reject it.

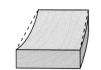

**BOW.** A warp on the face of a board from end to end. Unless the bow is severe, it can be easily straightened in the course of assembly.

**CUP.** A hollow across the face of a board. This is difficult to straighten out and is best avoided.

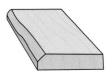

**WANE.** Missing wood or untrimmed bark along an edge. This is usually just a cosmetic problem.

**KNOTS.** Tight knots are not a problem, but large knots that are loose or have gouges will only get worse over time, and should be avoided in garden projects.

**CHECKING AND SPLITS.** A check is a crack that does not go all the way through; a split does. Both will probably grow worse over time.

**TWIST.** Multiple bends in a board. Twists are difficult to straighten out and are best avoided.

## Vertical and Flat Grain

Depending on how it was cut at the mill, a board may have vertical grain—narrow, parallel grain lines—or flat grain—wide lines that form wavy V shapes. Many boards have both types. Vertical-grain lumber is less likely to cup or twist and is stronger than flat-grain lumber. Whenever possible, choose boards with primarily vertical grain.

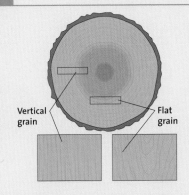

Vertical grain

Flat grain

# HAND TOOLS

BUILDING A TRELLIS OR ARBOR does not call for an expansive selection of tools. Most of the tools required are of the standard construction variety, so you may already have them—and any new tools you buy will likely be useful for future projects. These two pages discuss hand tools; for power tools, see pages 144–151.

## Carpentry Tools

A 25-foot tape measure will handle all your measuring needs. Check corners for square with a framing square. A smaller angle square is essential for marking cut lines on lumber and guiding the base of a circular saw. You may also need a T bevel to duplicate angles from one piece to another.

To check structures for level and plumb, a carpenter's level will do the job. A post level lets you check a post for plumb in both directions at once. Mason's line is used to establish straight lines when there are more than two posts in a row.

Even if you buy or rent a power nailer, a curved-claw hammer will be a constant companion, so buy one that is comfortable to use. A nailset is used to drive nails below the surface without marring the wood. A clamp or two can hold a rafter or other piece firmly and accurately in place while you drill holes or drive fasteners. For quick cuts, a handsaw is occasionally useful. Wood chisels are invaluable for cleaning out notches and completing cutouts. A flat pry bar helps you remove boards when you make a mistake and can pry crooked boards into place. A hand sanding block is often the fastest way to round off wooden edges.

Nailset

Post level

Clamp

Framing square

Carpenter's level

Sanding block

Wood chisel

Handsaw

T bevel

Curved
claw hammer

Angle square

Tape measure

Mason's line

Pry bar

## Digging Tools

If the digging is tough, you may want to
rent a power auger for postholes, but a
hand posthole digger will get the job
done in most cases. A digging bar cuts
through roots and pries loose rocks.
You may need a shovel or spade
to excavate sod.

Posthole digger

Digging bar

Shovel

# CUTTING TECHNIQUES

CHOOSE POWER CUTTING TOOLS THAT ARE UP TO THE TASK. A good-quality tool has plenty of power and feels stable as you work. There's no need to buy expensive pro-quality tools, but avoid the cheapest models, which can make it difficult to produce straight or smooth cuts.

## Measuring and Marking

Use a tape measure and angle square for most marking tasks. The hook end of the tape slides back and forth about $1/8$ inch so that inside measurements will be the same as outside measurements. To measure a board, slip the hook end over the end of the board, pull the tape along it, and draw a **V** mark with the tip at the spot to be cut. Use the angle square to draw a line through the **V**, and draw an **X** indicating the waste side of the line. Some carpenters draw the line through the middle of the measurement, indicating that the saw should cut through the middle of the line's thickness; others draw it just to the side, and then cut off the entire thickness of the line.

## Circular Saw

For most carpentry projects, no power tool sees more action than a circular saw. The most common style takes a $7^{1}/_{4}$-inch blade, which will cut to a depth of about $2^{1}/_{2}$ inches. A good-quality saw should be rated at more than 12 amps and uses ball or roller bearings rather than sleeve bearings.

Purchase at least one carbide-tipped blade with at least 24 teeth. Such a blade will last longer and produce smoother cuts than less expensive blades. When a blade starts to labor rather than glide during cutting, replace it or have it sharpened.

**A safe setup.** If the waste side of the cut is 2 feet or less, simply hang the board over the edge of a sawhorse or table and let the waste piece fall when you make the cut. A helper can also gently support the waste side to keep it from falling, but should never lift it up; doing so can cause the blade to bind. If the waste piece is longer than 2 feet (and therefore heavier), the board may crack and the saw may bind at the end of the cut. In that case, support the board in four places, as shown, so the board will remain stable during the cut.

**Check the blade for square.** If the blade is not square to the base of the saw, your cuts will be slightly beveled rather than square. Before cutting, unplug the saw, turn it upside down, retract the blade guard, and use a square to check the blade. For a more accurate test, cut two scrap boards and butt them together; if the ends do not meet precisely, the blade needs to be adjusted.

**Adjust the depth.** Before making a cut, unplug the saw and adjust the blade depth to about ¼ inch below the bottom of the board. It's easiest to make this adjustment with the saw on top of the board.

**Making a crosscut.** With practice you can achieve straight cuts freehand, but it's easy to make precision cuts if you use an angle square as a guide. Turn on the saw, barely begin to make the cut, and slide the square against the saw base plate. Hold it firm while you cut. The picture at right shows using an angle square to make a 45-degree cut.

**Making a rip cut.** To rip a board (that is, to cut it lengthwise), you could snap a chalk line and cut freehand, but it will be difficult to keep straight. Using a ripping guide (left), you can make rips nearly as precisely and quickly as you can with a table saw; this works well for making lattice pieces. You may need to nail or screw the board down so it does not move while you cut. If the board is narrow (for instance, when you are ripping the last few lattice slats from a board), the circular saw will tend to wobble. Place another board alongside the one you are cutting to provide a flat surface for the saw's base plate to rest on.

For quicker, less precise ripping, use the "finger guide" method (right): Start the cut, pinch the front inside edge of the base plate so that your finger slides along the board edge, then continue the cut.

## Table Saw

A portable table saw is the best tool for making long rip cuts, and is commonly used to produce lattice slats. For two or three hundred bucks you can buy a model with more than enough power and precision for the projects in this book. Or, rent a table saw from a home center.

**Setting up.** Some models have folding legs and set up in a few minutes. Alternatively, place the saw on a work table or attach it to a pair of sawhorses. Make sure the saw will not tilt easily when you push on it while cutting; some units have a special leg to keep this from happening.

It's important to support the board at the end of the cut. You can buy a special support with a roller, or simply position a sawhorse a few feet away and attach boards to it so it is the same height as the table saw. For a simpler solution, place the table saw on the ground and let the board end slide on the lawn when you reach the end of the cut.

**Set the fence.** For a rip cut, adjust the fence to the desired width. Measure to make sure that the fence is the same distance from the front and rear of the blade; otherwise, the saw can bind while you cut. Cut a scrap piece to make sure the width is correct and the blade will not bind.

**Check the kickback protection.** Most saws sold today have a small metal piece that keeps the board from kicking back when the board binds. If yours does not have this, purchase a featherboard, which can be clamped to the table to provide kickback protection.

**Making a rip cut.** Hold the board firmly against the fence and avoid wobbling or turning it as you feed it steadily through the blade. For a smooth cut, keep the board moving at all times; each time you start and stop, there will be visible saw marks. Ripping is easiest if you have a helper who can pull while you push. If the blade binds and stops turning, shut off the power right away. Lift up the kickback protectors, pull the board back a few inches, press the board firmly against the fence, and try again. If the motor shuts itself off, you may need to wait a few minutes and then push the reset button.

**Using a push stick.** Keep your fingers well away from the blade. When you near the end of a cut, use a small board, called a push stick, to finish the cut. This push stick has a notch cut in its end to make it easier to use. You can also buy plastic push sticks.

**Making a crosscut.** Crosscutting is not a table saw's strong suit, but with care you can make accurate 90-degree cuts. Check that the crosscut guide is set at precisely 90 degrees. Hold the board firmly against the guide, with your hands at least 6 inches away from the blade, and push the board through slowly.

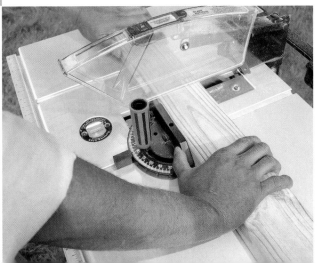

## Power Miter Saw

Many outdoor projects are built with only a circular saw. But a power miter saw, or chop saw, ensures straight cuts and clean joints. It makes short, neat work of miters and bevels. It can also dramatically speed up the process of cutting numerous lattice slats or top slats to identical lengths.

Anchor the chop saw on a stable, table-height surface. Provide blocks on each side to support the boards on each side. Some saws have a clamp that holds the lumber tight during cutting.

To test whether the saw is cutting accurately, cut two boards at identical 45-degree angles. Flip one of the boards 180 degrees and butt them together; they should align to create a straight board.

### TOOL OPTION

A hand miter saw works slowly, but can make very accurate cuts. It's well suited to narrow boards. Hold the board firmly against the fence while you cut.

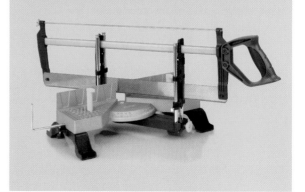

## Reciprocating Saw

A reciprocating saw can reach to cut in places a circular saw cannot reach, and it cuts more quickly than a handsaw. If you are cutting off or making a notch in a 6 by 6 post, for instance, first cut as much as you can with a circular saw, then finish with a reciprocating saw. It's not a good idea to use a reciprocating saw for visible portions of a cut, because it is hard to keep the blade straight.

When cutting with a reciprocating saw, sympathetic vibration is your enemy; if the piece is shaking while you are cutting, it will take a long time and the results will likely be ragged. If needed, have a helper hold the piece while you cut.

You can also use a reciprocating saw to surgically cut through hidden screws and nails. This makes it easier to dismantle mistakenly attached boards without damaging their surfaces.

## Cutting Decorative Rafter Ends

Rafter and beam ends that overhang an arbor are highly visible, so you may want to cut them to form a decorative pattern. Experiment with designs, using a compass or a paint can if the design calls for a curve or two. Once you have settled on a design, cut the first board and place it on top of each of the others as a template. Or, make a template out of cardboard or plywood. Use a circular saw to make as many of the cuts in each board as possible, taking care not to run the blade past the intersection of two lines. Use a jigsaw for any curved cuts and to finish where two straight cuts meet.

# ATTACHING BOARDS

TO ATTACH TWO BOARDS, YOU HAVE THREE BASIC OPTIONS: hand-nail, power-nail, or power-drive screws. On many projects you may employ two or even all three methods. Use fasteners that will not rust or corrode, such as decking or stainless-steel screws and double-dipped galvanized nails. Make sure the fasteners are approved for use with the type of treated lumber you are using (for example, ACQ or CA-B).

## Hand-Nailing

Driving nails by hand seems simple, but it takes practice to fully drive nails without bending them or marring the board. Practice on scraps until you are adept at avoiding mis-hits, which create frown- or smile-shaped indentations. Hold the hammer firmly, but allow your wrist to flex as you swing; it should feel natural and relaxed, and the hammer should have a little extra snap as it reaches the nail head. To make sure you do not indent the wood, use a nailset for the last blow. You can also use a nailset to recess the head of a finish nail slightly below the surface.

## Power-Nailing

Nowadays power-nailing is within the reach of a homeowner with a moderate budget. For about the same price as hiring a carpenter for a day, you can buy a kit that includes the compressor, hose, two finish nailers, and a stapler. For a little more, add a framing nailer as well.

With a power nailer you can consistently drive fasteners without damaging the wood; the nail holes are tiny. Another great advantage is that you can hold the piece in place with one hand while you drive with the other. And repetitive nailing—as when making lattice—goes four or five times faster than hand-nailing or power-driving screws.

Power finish nails are thin, so they do not hold as firmly as hand nails or screws. It's a good idea to drive two rather than one into a joint. Staples hold better than finish nails and produce only a slightly larger hole, so they are a good choice when making or attaching lattice.

To drive a power nail, press the tip of the nailer onto the wood until it retracts, then pull the trigger. You can also angle-drive nails (called "toe-nailing") this way. If the head is driven too deep or too shallow, adjust the compressor's pressure. Keep your hands well away from the nailing area because the nails sometimes wander, especially when they hit a knot. If you miss or a nail curves and sticks out, remove it with a pair of sliding-jaw pliers.

## The Importance of Pilot Holes

Whenever you drive a nail or screw within 3 inches of the end of a board, or through a thin or narrow board, there is a danger of splitting it. If you drill a pilot hole first, you will almost certainly avoid creating a crack. Pilot holes may seem like a hassle, but are well worth the small amount of time they require.

Use a drill bit that is slightly narrower than the screw or nail. The tool in the two photos below allows you to quickly change back and forth from a pilot screw to a drill bit. Or, if you have two drills, use one for drilling and the other one for driving screws. The pilot holes also countersink the screws, so the heads sit perfectly flush with the board.

When working near the ends of soft lumber, carpenters sometimes simply drill with the screwdriver bit to create a short "cheat" hole (above), then drive the screw. The faux pilot hole accommodates the screw head, which is more likely to crack the board than the screw's shaft.

## Carriage Bolts and Lag Screws

When installing a carriage bolt, drill a hole all the way through the lumber using a bit that is the same size as the bolt's shaft. For a lag screw, you could just drill a hole using a bit that is slightly smaller than the screw's shaft. To provide better insurance against splitting the board being attached, drill two holes as shown. The first hole is the same thickness as the screw's shaft.

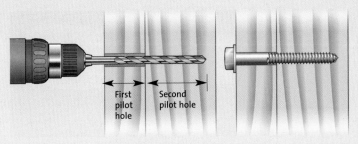

First pilot hole

Second pilot hole

# LATTICE WITH HALF-LAP JOINTS

YOU CAN MAKE A LATTICE PANEL by attaching vertical slats on top of horizontals (or vice versa), using a spacer to maintain consistent spacing (see page 45).

For tighter joints and a more crafted look, use half-lap joints. In this method, both verticals and horizontals are cut with a series of notches (or dadoes) that are the width of the lattice slats and half as deep as the slats' thickness. This allows the slats to fit together neatly, and the resulting trellis is the thickness of one slat rather than two.

If you are working with slats with sharp corners, aim to make the notches half the thickness, so the resulting lattice will be exactly one slat thick. When working with 1 by 2 or other material that has slightly rounded edges (as in these pages), it looks much better to cut the notches slightly shallower, so the lattice ends up being $\frac{1}{8}$ inch or so thicker than a slat.

**1** **LAY OUT FOR THE NOTCHES.** Determine the spacing you want between the slats. If the lattice panel must fit in a predetermined space, you will need to experiment to find the correct spacing. Use a scrap of lattice slat to help draw pairs of lines for each slat.

**2** **CUT THE LINES.** Set a circular saw to cut about halfway through the thickness of the slats. Cut a scrap piece and measure the depth to be sure. Then, using the circular saw method shown on page 153, cut and clear out notches on two scrap pieces and press them together to test the fit for both width and depth. Use the circular saw to cut the lines on each side of the marked notches.

**3** **ADJUST THE ROUTER DEPTH.** Set a router to cut to the same depth as the circular saw cuts, and test it on a scrap board.

**4** **CLEAR OUT THE GROOVES.** Use the router equipped with a straight-cutting bit to clean out the spaces between the cuts. Hold the router firmly, to keep it from wandering outside the notches.

## TOOL OPTION

If you do not have a router, use a circular saw to clean out the notches. You may need to retract the blade guard as you make repeated cuts.

**5** **TEST THE FIT.** Because material can vary slightly in width, and because everyone makes cutting mistakes, dry-fit all the pieces before actually attaching them. You may need to use a circular saw to widen some of the notches slightly. The pieces should fit fairly snugly, but not so tightly that you have to pound hard with a hammer to put them together.

**6** **DISASSEMBLE AND APPLY GLUE.** Remove three or four pieces. Apply dabs of glue in each of the notches.

**7** **NAIL OR STAPLE.** Replace the slats and tap with a hammer as needed to make a tight joint. Drive short nails or staples into each joint. Repeat for all the joints. Avoid moving the lattice for an hour, or however long is recommended on the glue's label.

# SETTING POSTS

IN MOST CASES, ARBOR POSTS SHOULD BE POSITIONED IN A RECTANGLE, WITH 90-DEGREE CORNERS. If you set the posts in concrete you will increase the structure's rigidity. However, posts set in a deep hole (32 inches or deeper) and backfilled with well-tamped soil or gravel will be nearly as strong. An informal structure like an arbor is not expected to be very strong, so you may choose to set into shallow holes, thought it may sway a bit if people lean on it.

## Check for Utility Lines

You probably have all sorts of pipes and cables running under your yard. A posthole dug deeper than a foot may run into a utility line, and digging even a shallow hole may cause you to break into a sprinkler line.

Cutting into a gas, water, or electrical line can be expensive and dangerous. Contact your gas, electric, and water companies to learn the locations of their lines. A company may come out and mark the lines with a series of little flags. Sprinkler lines are not mapped, but you can often figure out their paths by looking at sprinkler heads and connecting the dots. If you do cut through a sprinkler line, the repair will take a bit of time, but will not be difficult.

## Laying Out

For a fence-like trellis with more than two posts, dig holes and set the outer posts, then stretch lines between them to lay out for the positions of the intermediate posts. For a set of four posts in a rectangle, take a bit of time to get them in the correct arrangement.

You can measure for the positions of the postholes, but it's safer to lay the arches or other top pieces on the ground. Start to dig one pair of holes. Drive stakes in the middle of the posts. Measure to mark for a pair of holes that are parallel (right, top). Then measure the diagonals to make sure the holes form a rectangle, with 90-degree corners (right, bottom).

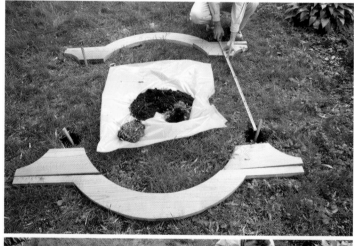

## Digging Holes

If the soil cooperates, digging four holes can be less than an hour's work. However, soil that has a high clay content, large rocks, or thick roots can turn digging into a major project.

In most cases, a hand-operated posthole digger will be up to the job. Slice through the sod, pull it up in a chunk, and set it aside so you can later use it to fill in around the post. If the hole will be only 2 feet deep, you can make the hole only as wide as the digger's jaws. If the hole will be bigger, you'll need to widen the hole so you can pull the handles apart as the hole deepens.

If you encounter a root, you may be able to chop through it with the digger or a shovel. If the root is thick, cut through it with a digging bar or a reciprocating saw. To remove a large rock, loosen it with a digging bar, then extract it with the posthole digger.

To ease the task of digging holes, consider renting a power auger. Some models are operated by a single person, but a two-person auger works better when digging a large hole or when working in difficult soil.

**MATERIALS TIP**

For a modest project, consider anchoring the post with a pound-in anchor. Use a sledgehammer and a wood block to drive the anchor, taking care that it is facing the right direction. Slip the post into the anchor, and drive screws to fasten the post.

## Setting Posts

A post rated for ground contact can withstand plenty of moisture, but there's no sense in tempting fate: Take steps to keep rainwater from puddling around the post or settling into the bottom of the hole. It is common to set pressure-treated posts in holes filled with well-tamped soil, but if conditions are wet you may want to use gravel instead.

Shovel 3 inches or so of gravel into the bottom of the hole, and use the post to tamp it firm. This will allow water to drain away from the bottom of the post.

Place the posts in the ground and check that they are facing the right way, so boards attached to their sides will lie flat against the posts. Use a post level to check a post for plumb in both directions at once.

Shovel in about a foot of soil and use a board to tamp it firm. Repeat the process until you reach the top of the hole. Mound the soil up 2 inches or so above ground level and tamp it at an angle so rainwater will run away from the post.

When installing a cedar post, which is not as rot-resistant as treated lumber, fill the hole with gravel rather than soil, tamping as you go.

For the greatest rigidity, set posts in concrete, as shown on page 106.

## Cutting Posts

In most cases, it's easier to cut posts to height after they are set. Otherwise, you would need to dig all the holes to exact depths.

Use a carpenter's level, or a level set atop a board, to mark all the posts for cutting at the same height. On each post, use an angle square to draw lines all around the post. Check that the blade of your circular saw is square (see page 145). Get into a comfortable position

and hold the saw's base plate flat against the post as you cut one line. Then cut the line on the opposite side.

# FINISHING

ONCE THE ARBOR OR TRELLIS IS BUILT AND INSTALLED, take the time to add finishing touches that will make it splinter- and rot-free as well as more attractive.

## Sanding and Routing

A hand sander may be all you need to slightly round off cut edges. Use 80- or 100-grit sandpaper, and whenever possible work in long, sweeping strokes rather than short, choppy strikes. When sanding an edge, run the sander at an angle, rather than parallel to the edge. For more heavy-duty work, use a random-orbit palm sander. Use a belt sander only if you have a lot of material to remove.

Practice on scrap pieces. Some woods sand quickly, and with these you'll need to take precautions against digging in; harder boards are virtually impossible to oversand. As you sand, keep the tool moving and hold the sandpaper flat against the edge; stopping in one place or tilting the tool could cause it to dig in.

A router equipped with a roundover bit produces a more uniform version of a sanded corner. You can also use an ogee bit to create an ornate edge. Edging bits have self-guiding tips that glide along the board's edge. Practice on scrap pieces until you get the depth you desire. Hold the router's base plate flat on the board, with the bit in midair an inch or so away from the edge. Turn on the router, slide it toward the board until the bit starts cutting, and move the router along the edges using smooth motions. Always keep the base plate flat on the board, and you should be fine.

## Choosing Finishes

To protect a structure and preserve its beauty, apply a water repellent (sealer) and a semitransparent or solid-color stain, or primer and paint. Try the product on a sample board first and always read the label. Some products should not be applied to new wood, and some may require a sealer first.

**Sealers and stains.** Sealers, also called water repellents, help avoid warping and cracking. They may be clear or slightly tinted (in which case you could think of them as a sealer/stain). A clear sealer does not protect the wood from the ultraviolet part of sunlight, so the wood will gradually turn gray. The only way to keep wood from going gray is to add at least a little amount of tinting. (Products labeled as clear with "UV protection" or "UV blocking" do change the color of the wood, at least slightly.) If your site is damp or if termites are a problem, get a product that also contains a mildewcide, an insecticide, or both.

Water-base sealers do a good job, but oil-base sealers last longer; you may need to reapply a water-base product every year, and an oil-base product every other year.

Do not use film-forming finishes like spar varnish or polyurethane outdoors. They wear quickly and are difficult to renew.

Semitransparent stains contain enough pigment to tint the wood with one coat while letting the grain show through. Some are formulated for use with pressure-treated wood: they have a bit more red tint to overcome the wood's greenish hue. The effect varies depending on how green the wood is; experiment on scrap pieces.

**Paints.** Paints hide defects so thoroughly that they let you use lower grades of lumber. Modern latex exterior paint is now generally considered superior to alkyd- or oil-base paints for most applications.

Before applying paint, apply primer, both to keep colors from knots, pressure treatment, and other sources from bleeding through, and to ensure that the paint will stick and not peel or bubble. Primers may have an alkyd, oil, latex, or alcohol base.

## Pre-Painting

Painting, or at least priming, lattice slats and other pieces before the project is assembled can save you time in the long run, and can result in a neater job too. Do this only if the wood is dry enough.

Place the pieces on scraps of thin wood over a drop cloth. Apply the paint in long, smooth strokes to two or three sides. After painting six or seven pieces, go back over them to brush away any globs or drips. Once dry, turn the pieces over and finish painting. Touch up the places where paint rests on the scrap pieces.

## Painting and Staining

Wait for treated wood to dry before applying sealer and stain or primer and paint. To test, sprinkle a bit of water on a horizontal surface. If the water soaks in, you can proceed; if it beads up, wait a week and test again.

If you apply the finish with a brush, be on the lookout for drips and runs, especially when brushing crisscrossed pieces. On flat surfaces, try applying the finish first with a small roller, then immediately following up with a brush.

Perhaps the best way to finish a structure with interlacing pieces is to use a paint sprayer. Buy an inexpensive model or rent a professional-quality sprayer. Spray on a thin coat to prevent drips, and allow the paint to dry before spraying several more coats. Have a brush handy to smooth out drips.

---

**PRO TIP**

If an existing structure has turned gray and you want a stained look, use a stiff brush to scrub the wood with a mixture of two parts water to one part household bleach, or a solution of wood bleach (oxalic acid) mixed according to the package directions. Upon drying, the wood should turn a light blond color. (If it doesn't, wash it again.) Now you can apply the stain of your choice.

# ACKNOWLEDGMENTS

## PHOTOGRAPHY CREDITS

Unless otherwise credited, all photos are by Steve Cory and Diane Slavik. (T = top; L = left; M = middle; B = bottom; R = right) **Richard Bloom/photolibrary.com:** 130TM; **Marion Brenner:** 19T; **Brian Vanden Brink:** 25T; **Rob D. Brodman:** 9BR; **F. Buffetrille/M.A.P.:** 4B; **Karen Bussolini:** 59B; **Rob Cardillo:** 47BL; **David Cavagnaro:** 21B, 120R; **Van Chaplin/SPC Photo Collection:** 17T, 23T; **Torie Chugg/The Garden Collection:** 12TL; **Claire Curran:** 27T, 29, 130R; **Robin B. Cushman:** 8TL, 16BR, 44, 128B; **Alan & Linda Detrick:** 50, 68, 135TL; **Andrew Drake:** 9BL, 11B, 27B; **Liz Eddison/The Garden Collection:** 20M; **Elena Elisseeva/Big Stock Photo:** 12BR; **Catriona Tudor Erler:** 15R, 16BL, 20T, 96; **Richard Felber:** 6BL; **Cheryl Fenton:** 33M, 33R (3), 140BL, 142 (3), 143 (1); **Scott Fitzgerrell:** 138 (3), 139M, 142 (1), 143 (6), 148B, 157B, 158B; **Roger Foley:** 10B, 18B, 30 (main), 34, 36, 57 all, 67 all, 93–95 all, 97–99 all, 101–103 all, 109–111 all, 132B; **John Glover:** 66; **John Glover/photolibrary.com:** 6BR; **Jay Graham:** 72BM, 88T; **Steven Gunther:** 28BL, 135TM; **Philip Harvey:** 143; **Saxon Holt:** 6, 16T, 28BR, 76, 114, 118BL, 118 (main), 124, 133; **Melissa Jones/©istockphoto.com:** 4T; **Lynn Karlin:** 42T, 52B; **Andrew Lawson:** 1, 10T; **Janet Loughrey:** 8B, 15B, 15T, 48TL; **Allan Mandell:** 104; **Charles Mann:** 53T, 55B, 119BR, 129TL; **Sylvia Martin/SPC Picture Collection:** 5; 112–113 all; **N. & P. Mioulane/M.A.P.:** 92; **Terrence Moore:** 14; **Courtesy of New England Arbors:** 74; **Courtesy of Oasis™ Decking by Alcoa:** 140TL; **Jerry Pavia:** 3B, 6BM, 11T, 21T, 22B, 40T, 46TL, 56, 125BL, 126TL, 126TR, 127 all, 128T, 129TR, 131B, 132TL, 138TL; **Pam Peirce/Susan A. Roth & Co.:** 53B; **Norm Plate:** 17B, 49B; **Cheryl R. Richter:** 73BR, 100; **John Rizzo:** 62; **Lisa Romerein:** 13, 22T, 24, 25B, 40B, 135BL; **Susan A. Roth:** 9T, 19B, 26T, 118BR, 125TL, 126B, 128R, 134; **Mark Rutherford:** 148T, 155BL; **David Schiff:** 142 (3), 143 (1); **Evan Sklar/JupiterImages.com:** 18T; **Courtesy of Smith & Hawken:** 33B, 75BL, 75BR; **Derek St Romaine/The Garden Collection:** 2B; **Charles Stirling/Alamy Limited:** 132TR; **Thomas J. Story:** 143; **F. Strauss/M.A.P.:** 30BM, 60; **Michael S. Thompson:** 26B, 130L, 130BM; **Courtesy of Trex Company, Inc.:** 140TL; **Nance S. Trueworthy:** 108; **Mark Turner:** 12BL, 12TR, 38, 117B, 128L, 131T; **Juliette Wade/gardenpicture.com:** 54L; **Deidra Walpole:** 3T, 23B, 72 (main), 80, 84, 120L; **Courtesy of Walpole Woodworkers:** 2T, 7BR, 32L, 159; **Rick Wetherbee:** 135BR; **Judy White/GardenPhotos.com:** 28T, 59T, 125BR, 129B, 132BL; **Russ Widstrand:** 20B; **Bob Wigand:** 49TL, 58, 135TR; **Martha Woodward:** 123TL; **Courtesy of Woodway Products:** 140R

## DESIGN CREDITS

**1:** David Wheeler and Simon Dorrell; **2B:** Lloyd Christie—RHS Chelsea 1998; **8TL:** Leann Olson; **9T:** Conni Cross; **9BR:** Steve and Sue Loy with Jim Lord Landscape Services; **10B:** Chapel Valley Landscape Co.; **10T:** David Wheeler and Simon Dorrell; **12BL:** Elmer and JoAnne Roose; **12TR:** Terry Lehmann; **14:** Scott Calhoun, ZonaGardens; **15B:** Charlie Atwood-King & Karen Lamitie-King; **15T:** Roger and Joann Thomas; **16T:** Freeland Tanner; **17B:** Bob Riebe and Buster Brewer; **18B:** Chapel Valley Landscape Co.; **19B:** North Hill; **19T:** Shelly Coglizer and Ron Lutsko, Lutsko Associates Landscape; **20M:** Butler Landscapes—Tatton Park 2002; **22T:** Tom and Juliette Domenici; **26T:** Kristin Horne; **27B:** David Pfeiffer, Garden Architecture, Inc.; **27T:** Summers Past Farms; **28BL:** Jan and Skip Tschantz; **30 (main) and 36:** Clinton and Associates; **44:** John Kaib; **48TL:** Thomas Vetter; **49B:** Ten Eyck Landscape Architects; **59B:** John Scofield; **62:** Kelman and Kirsten Acres; **68:** Debbie and John VanBourgondien; **72 (main):** Ruby Begonia Fine Gardens Design; **76:** Freeland Tanner; **80:** Ruby Begonia Fine Gardens Design; **84:** Mayita Dinos Garden Design; **96:** Leonora R. Burnet and Douglas King Burnet; **114:** Michael Bates; **117B:** Cathy and Mike Walker; **118 (main):** Steven Antonow; **118BR and 125TL:** Gail Gee; **128L:** Julie Mahoney; **131T:** VanDusen Botanical Garden; **132BR:** Yunghi Choi; **134:** Bartholdi Park/U.S. Botanic Garden

## PRODUCT RESOURCES

**Arboria**
arboria.com
1-800-459-8718
*Quality garden structures and hardwood furniture*

**New England Arbors**
newenglandarbors.com
1-866-325-1065
*Durable and attractive low-maintenance vinyl arbors*

**Smith & Hawken**
smithandhawken.com
1-800-940-1170
*Metal and cedar garden structures, plus plants and gardening tools*

**Walpole Woodworkers**
walpolewoodworkers.com
1-800-343-6948
*Handcrafted wood, vinyl, and iron outdoor structures*

**Woodway Products**
woodwayproducts.com
1-800-459-8718
*High-quality lattice, solid wood planking, deck railing, and post caps*

# INDEX

Page numbers in **boldface** refer to photographs.